MW01640270

Thank you for
Choosing Orlando to
host your GameTech Confe
I wish you the utmost succe
for your event and hope you
enjoy your time in Orlando!

Jessica Jacobs

HISTORIC ORANGE COUNTY

The Story of Orlando and Orange County

Commissioned by the Orange Rounty Regional History Center.

Historical Publishing Network
A division of Lammert Incorporated
San Antonio, Texas

A railroad station in the town of Maitland, c.1900.
COURTESY OF THE ORANGE COUNTY REGIONAL HISTORY CENTER.

First Edition

ISBN: 9781893619999
Library of Congress Card Catalog Number: 2009925988

Historic Orange County: The Story of Orlando and Orange County

authors: Tana Mosier Porter, Ph.D.
Cassandra Fyotek
Stephanie Gaub
Barbara Knowles
Garret Kremer-Wright
Cynthia Cardona Meléndez
cover artist: Lu Halstead Tieman
contributing writer for "Sharing the Heritage": Joe Goodpasture

Historical Publishing Network
president: Ron Lammert
project manager: Wynn Buck
administration: Donna M. Mata
Melissa Quinn
book sales: Dee Steidle
production: Colin Hart
Glenda Tarazon Krouse
Craig Mitchell
Roy Arellano
Charles A. Newton, III
Evelyn Hart

Contents

Foreword

From Apopka to Zellwood, the histories of Orange County's communities tell the history of the county itself. The communities came first, some of them when the vast unknown region was still Mosquito County. County boundaries changed, but the communities grew and multiplied. A dozen incorporated cities, an equal number of populated unincorporated towns, and innumerable smaller places make up the Orange County of today.

HISTORIC ORANGE COUNTY tells the story of Orange County and its communities from the time the first Spanish explorers stepped ashore to its emergence as one of the world's favorite tourist destinations. Tracing its growth from colonial and territorial days through the Seminole Wars, the book examines Orange County's slow growth before the railroads solved its transportation dilemma, its rise to the top of the citrus industry in the early years of the twentieth century, and its population explosion during the Florida Land Boom of the 1920s. The book highlights the accomplishments of the people who created the communities that make up Orange County, from Aaron Jernigan and his brother Isaac, David Mizell, Judge Speer, and other early pioneers, cattleman Jacob Summerlin, citrus innovator Dr. P. Phillips, and aerospace manufacturer Glenn Martin, to Walt Disney. Nearly two hundred years of the county's past come alive in the words and pictures of Historic Orange County.

Orange County

BY TANA MOSIER PORTER

Millions of years ago, during the Ice Age, glaciers spread over much of North America. The glaciers did not reach Florida, but the freezing and thawing of the thick ice cover caused the ocean level to rise and fall, alternately flooding and exposing the land to create the Floridian Plateau. Florida's shape, size, and coastline evolved during this process. The remnants of the beaches and sand dunes remained in the center of the peninsula, north of Lake Okeechobee and west of the St. Johns River, as a series of north-south ridges known as the Central Florida Highlands. Most of Florida's eight thousand lakes are found in the Central Highlands, where the porous limestone underlying the soil collapses to create sinkholes, which then fill with water.

Mammoths, not tourists, once roamed Central Florida.

COURTESY OF THE ORANGE COUNTY REGIONAL HISTORY CENTER.

Orange County's location on the Orlando Ridge in the geographical Central Florida Highlands played a determining role in its history and economic development. The level prairie and abundant water drew cattlemen with their herds. Citrus groves flourished in the sandy, well-drained soils. The subtropical climate attracted tourists, and the prevalence of perfect flying days eventually brought the aviation industry. Despite the terms "plateau" and "highlands," no place in Orange County exceeds Windermere's elevation of 150 feet above sea level.

The first humans came to Florida more than 12,000 years ago, migrating south away from the cold. The nomadic Paleo people hunted the mastodons, mammoths, and saber-toothed tigers that roamed the peninsula during the Ice Age. The animals eventually disappeared, but the people stayed. Evidence suggests that Paleo people hunted along Orange County's Lake Apopka and Wekiva River as early as nine thousand years ago. About sixt thousand years ago the land began to warm and Archaic people appeared. More advanced than the Paleo people, they learned to make pottery to store food, enabling them to live in villages and cultivate crops. Pottery found in Orange County indicates that the Archaic people lived in the region more than three thousand years ago.

As many as a half-million Native Americans populated parts of the peninsula when the first Spaniards came ashore, among them the Apalachee, Tekesta, Calusa, Ai, and the Timucua, who occupied parts of the Central Highlands and hunted in Orange County. Unknown numbers of Indians died fighting wars against the European explorers and as a result of Spanish attempts to enslave them, but the Native Americans suffered most from contagious diseases brought by the invaders. Whole villages died from smallpox, measles, and mumps because the European illnesses were new to the Indians and they had no immunity to them. By the beginning of the nineteenth

Above: *A typical Timucuan village.*

COURTESY OF THE STATE ARCHIVES OF FLORIDA.

Below: *A 1564 map of Florida.*

COURTESY OF THE ORANGE COUNTY REGIONAL HISTORY CENTER.

century Florida's indigenous peoples had completely disappeared.

Christopher Columbus and other explorers probably visited the peninsula earlier, but Ponce de León, who landed near St. Augustine in 1513 in search of gold, treasure, and the Fountain of Youth, gets official credit for the European discovery of Florida. He claimed the land for Spain, naming it La Florida, meaning Land of Flowers. Spaniard Pedro Menéndez de Avilés established the first successful European community at St. Augustine in 1565.

Spain kept possession of Florida for more than two hundred years before giving it up to Great Britain in 1763 as part of the settlement ending the French and Indian War. In 1784, at the end of the American Revolution, Spain reclaimed Florida but found it impossible to maintain order in the distant colony. After lengthy negotiations and some opposition in Congress, the United States purchased Florida from Spain, and the American flag replaced the Spanish flag at Pensacola on July 17, 1821. The Spanish and the British established successful communities in northern Florida but none in present-day Orange County. In fact, few people besides Native Americans had even seen the central part of the peninsula when Florida became a United States territory. John Randolph of Roanoke, arguing in Congress against the purchase of Florida, declared that, "No man would immigrate into Florida...a land of swamps, of quagmires, of frogs and alligators and mosquitoes."

Andrew Jackson, Florida's first territorial governor, organized the territory in 1821, setting up a civil government and creating two counties: Escambia and St. Johns. The territorial legislature created two more counties in 1822 and two in 1823. In 1824 the number of Florida's counties nearly

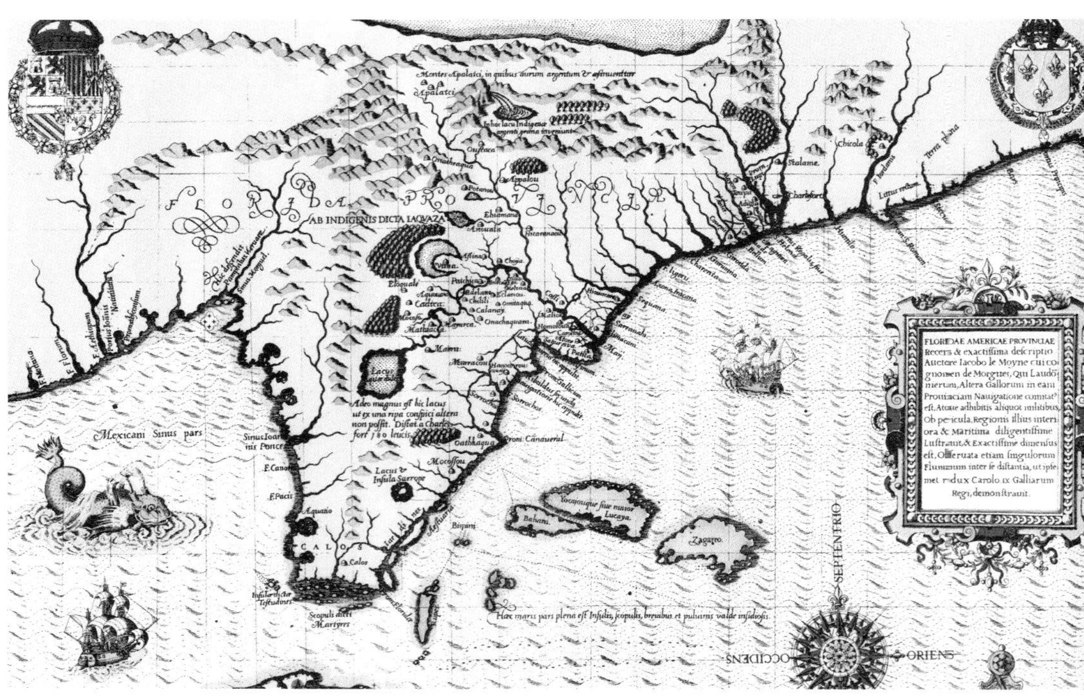

doubled, with five established on December 29, including Mosquito, the eleventh county and the only one named for an insect. Taken from St. Johns County, Mosquito included parts of what are now Flagler, Marion, Lake, Brevard, Indian River, St. Lucie, Martin, Orange, Palm Beach, Volusia, and Seminole Counties.

Three main issues confronted the territorial government: internal improvements, land ownership, and Indian affairs. Before public land could be sold it had to be surveyed and Spanish land grants settled. The surveying began in 1824. As specified in the Ordinance of 1785, the land was surveyed in sections, townships, and ranges beginning with the north-south Tallahassee meridian and a surveyed baseline running east and west. Most of Florida is surveyed into one-mile squares of 640 acres each. Each square is a section, and thirty-six sections make a township. Despite Indian hostilities, surveyors completed much of Central Florida during the territorial period, though until the end of the Second Seminole War few settlers ventured south of a line from the Tampa Bay to St. Augustine.

Governmental authority rested with the courts rather than the county governments, and beginning in 1823, a court in each county covered administrative as well as judicial responsibilities. Mosquito and St. Johns Counties shared the same representative in the legislative council until 1835, and no record seems to exist of a county seat until Charles Downing, Mosquito County's first representative, introduced a bill in 1835 to make New Smyrna the county seat. However, the county records remained at St. Augustine until 1843. Mosquito County became a Superior Court district in 1844.

Mosquito County then included territory from Matanzas Inlet south to Jupiter Inlet. The county boundary continued west along the southern shore of Lake Okeechobee and north along the Indian Reservation. According to John Lee Williams, who published a history of the Florida Territory in 1837, "Musquito" County was 190 miles long and 60 miles wide, with the population concentrated around New Smyrna and St. Augustine. "The balance of the county is unsettled," Williams noted. "No person has penetrated the country, many miles west of Indian River."

The territorial legislature reduced Mosquito County's original 7,000 square miles in 1828, when it ceded 1,200 square miles to the Seminole Indians for a reservation. Florida's Indians had died from European diseases during the sixteenth and seventeenth centuries, but in the eighteenth century, as white settlement in the southern states overran traditional Indian homelands, the Creek and Miccosukee Indians began to move from Georgia, Tennessee, and the Carolinas south into Florida. They became known collectively as Seminoles, from a Spanish word meaning "renegade," and the runaway slaves and free blacks who lived with

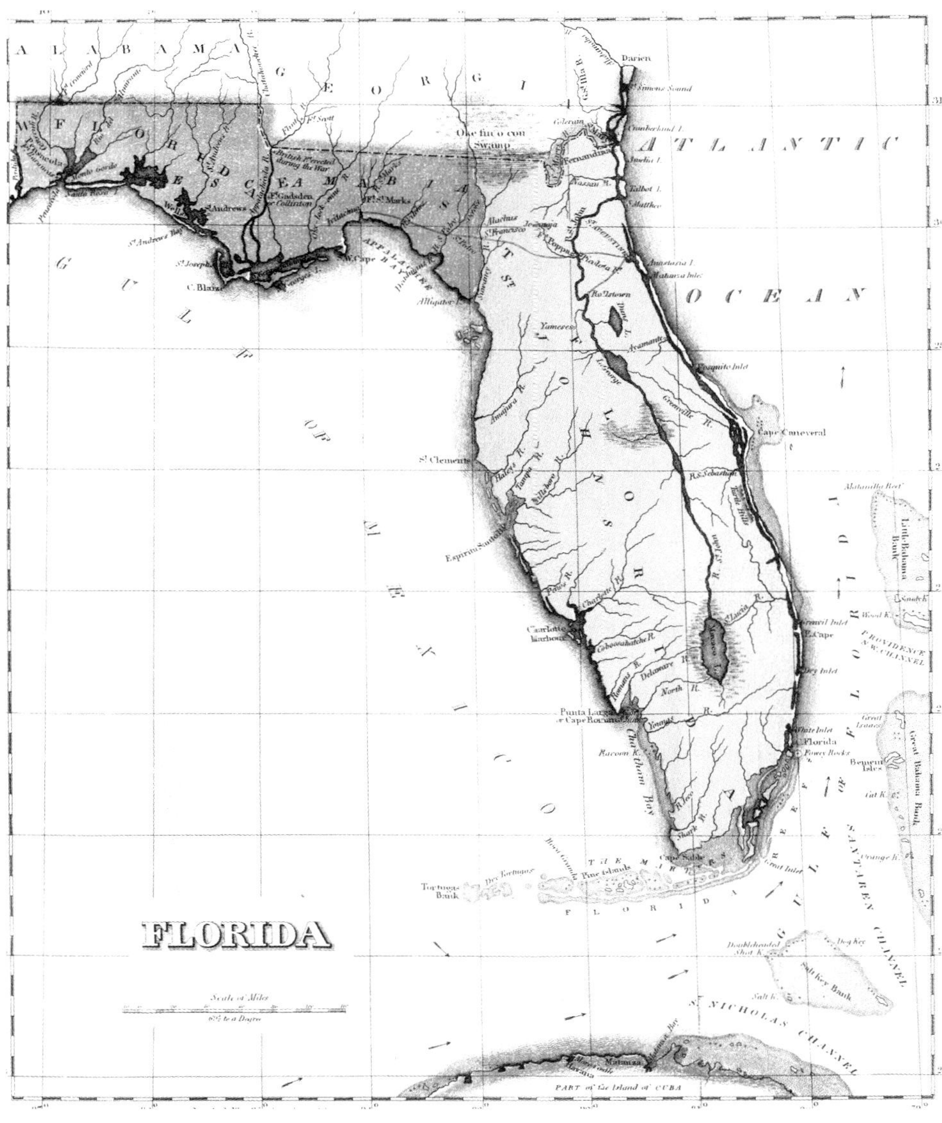

An 1822 map of Florida.

COURTESY OF THE ORANGE COUNTY REGIONAL HISTORY CENTER

them became known as Black Seminoles. The Black Seminoles complicated the Indian question in Florida, where whites feared both Indian attacks and slave uprisings. Before 1832 Florida had no official policy toward the Indians, though the territorial government occupied much of its time considering how to remove them from Florida. The determination of the Seminoles to remain in Central Florida slowed development of the region.

Responding to national agitation, Congress passed the Indian Removal Act of 1835, which required that all Native Americans in the United States and its territories move to Indian Territory west of the Mississippi River. The Seminoles refused to go. They did not want to leave Florida, and they would not abandon the Black Seminoles or allow them to become plantation slaves. The United States fought three wars against the Seminoles and their allies, the first in 1818 and 1819, before Florida became a U.S. territory. The second and the third, from 1835 to 1842 and from 1849 until 1856, were failed attempts to remove every Seminole from Florida.

The Second Seminole War led to the settlement of Orange County. Fought in Central Florida, home of the Seminole Chief Osceola, it began in 1835 with Dade's Massacre near Bushnell. The Black Seminole leader, Negro Abraham, led a surprise attack on a company of U.S. troops led by General Dade, killing nearly every soldier. Skirmishes followed at Lake Apopka in 1837 and at the Black Seminole town of Peliklakaha near Lake Apopka in 1842.

The Indian fighting style of sneak attacks and short skirmishes, combined with a complete absence of wagon roads or even trails in unsettled Central Florida, forced the

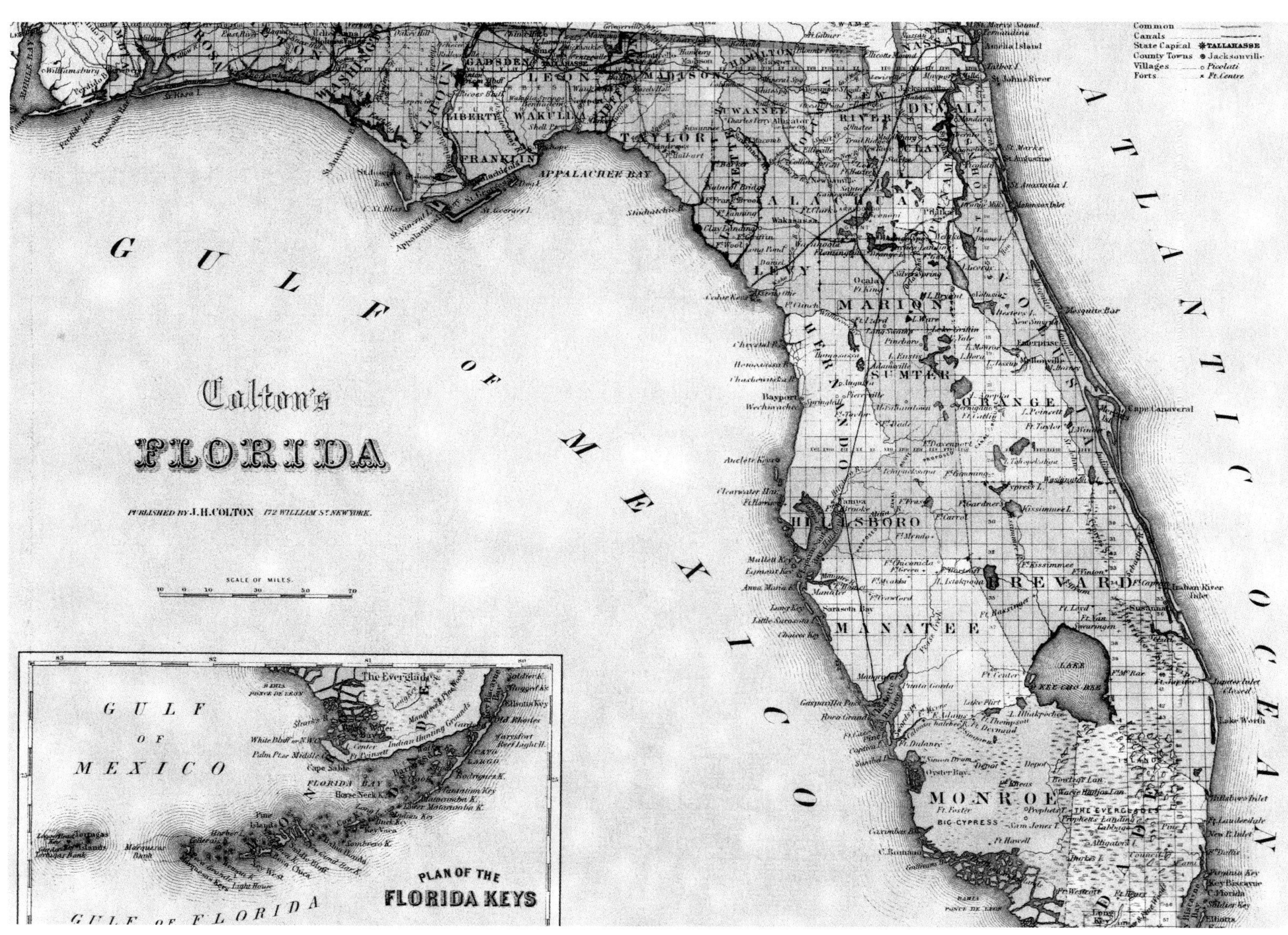

An 1855 map of Florida.

COURTESY OF THE ORANGE COUNTY REGIONAL HISTORY CENTER.

army to develop a new style of warfare. The soldiers had to clear their way through the cypress swamps, pine barrens and palmetto, building roads and bridges as they went. Supply wagons could not keep up as the army moved south. Adopting a new tactic, the army built a series of forts thirty miles apart in a line running south along the St. Johns River and west along the Indian trail from Lake Monroe to the Tampa Bay. The forts protected the military wagons struggling through Central Florida and served as supply depots for troops isolated along the frontier. Ten of the forts were in Mosquito County, with three in present-day Orange County: Fort Christmas, constructed in 1837, and Forts Maitland and Gatlin, both built in 1838.

When the Second Seminole War ended in 1842, the United States government offered land under the Armed Occupation Act to anyone who would settle near the forts and act as citizen soldiers. The homesteaders would occupy the former Indian land and become soldiers in the event of Indian uprisings along the frontier between the new settlements and the Seminoles, now relocated to reservations further south. Many soldiers who fought in the Seminole War returned to live in the area. Military maps and roads, along with free land, brought pioneers to Orange County for the first time.

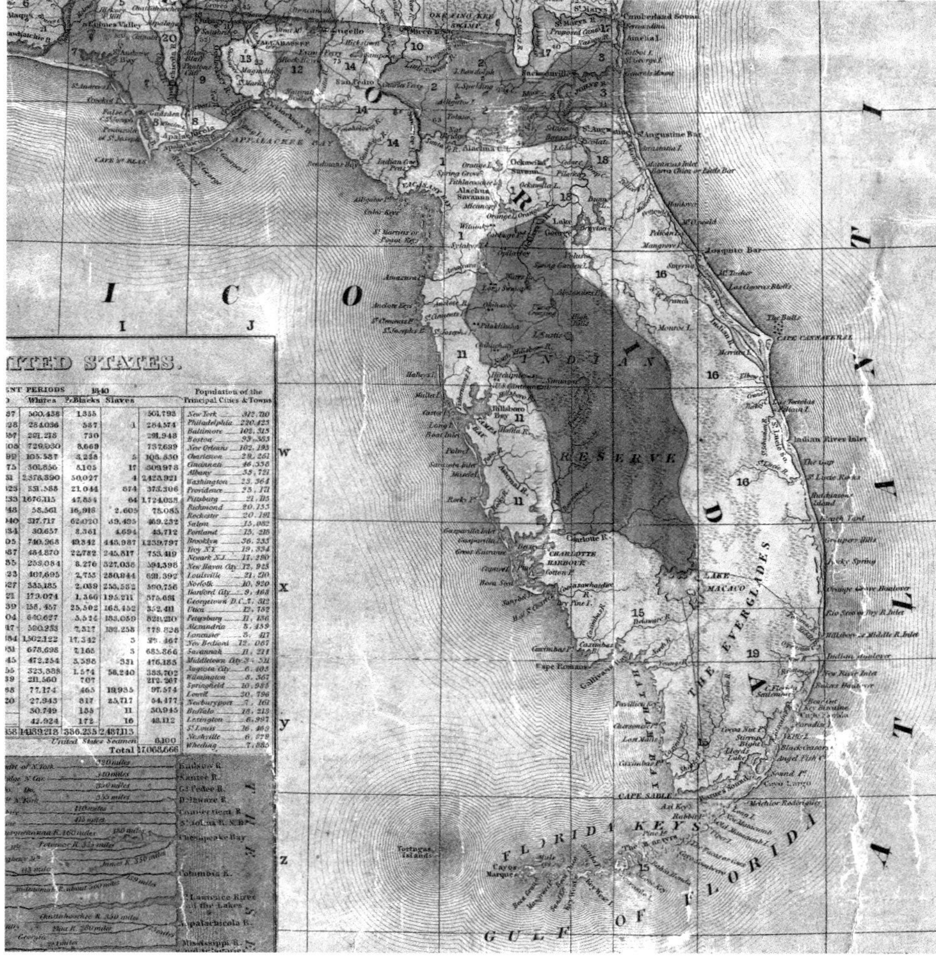

Among the first settlers in Central Florida, Vincent Lee acquired land on the Wekiva River, and Henry A. Crane settled near Fort Mellon in November 1842. Dr. A.S. Speer went to Fort Reed, south of Sanford. The first to settle in what is now Orange County, Aaron Jernigan and his brother Isaac arrived in the summer of 1842, bringing cattle and slaves. They established homes near Fort Gatlin, on Lake Holden, south of Orlando. In December of 1842, Vincent Lee purchased property south of present-day Orlando. Others followed, and a community called Jernigan developed by 1850, when a post office opened in Jernigan's house. James M. Janney and William J. Morgan settled near Lake Apopka in 1843, probably taking out the first homestead permits for the Apopka area.

With the Seminole War seemingly ended, some Floridians urged early statehood. Mosquito County's representative, W. H. Williams, signed a protest, however, opposing statehood and joining a group from St.

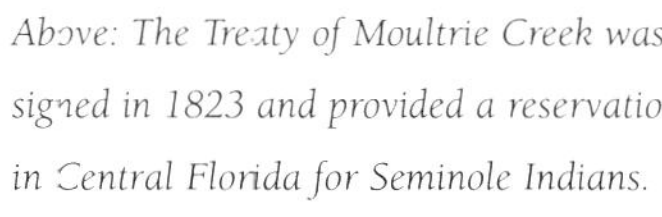

Above: The Treaty of Moultrie Creek was signed in 1823 and provided a reservation in Central Florida for Seminole Indians.

COURTESY OF THE ORANGE COUNTY REGIONAL HISTORY CENTER.

Left: Seminole chief Osceola.

COURTESY OF THE ORANGE COUNTY REGIONAL HISTORY CENTER.

Augustine who preferred the division of Florida into two states: East Florida and West Florida. Since such a division would have created two slave states and changed the balance of slave to free states, the argument for division was an argument against statehood at that time.

A painting depicting Dade's Massacre of the Second Seminole War.

COURTESY OF THE DADE BATTLEFIELD SOCIETY, INC.

In January 1842, a bill to "alter the name of Mosquito County" passed both houses of the legislative council and was assumed to have become law. However, the proposal to change the name to Leigh Read County to honor a Seminole War hero had stalled on the desk of a clerk, who may have been one of a number of people who opposed the change. The hero had been challenged to a duel in Tallahassee, had killed his man, and was in turn shot and killed by the brother of his dueling opponent, who escaped. The governor did not receive the bill for his signature during the time required, and thus the proposal did not become law. Another bill submitted and signed before the session ended reinstated the name Mosquito County.

Cornelius Taylor, the representative from Mosquito County, tried again in 1843, this time suggesting Carroll County, to honor Sergeant Francis Carroll, also a hero of the Seminole War, but he introduced no formal bill. His bill to move the county seat from New Smyrna to Enterprise, where he owned a plantation, became law in February 1843. County residents cast forty-four votes in the November election that year.

On January 30, 1845, the Legislative Council passed a bill changing the name of the county from Mosquito to Orange, probably taking the name from the orange trees, or possibly from the Orange Mounds Indian site on the St. Johns River northeast of Fort Christmas. Florida entered the Union as the twenty-seventh state on March 3, 1845. Orange County elected Aaron Jernigan to be its first state representative. The state legislature made Mellonville, now Sanford, county seat of Orange County on July 16, 1845, and it remained so until December 30, 1856, when the electorate voted to move the seat of the county government to the settlement near Fort Gatlin.

Statehood made little change in Central Florida. The citizen soldiers who homesteaded near the military forts were called upon to defend their settlements against the Indians in the Third Seminole War, from 1849 until 1856. Aaron Jernigan's daughter later told of being "forted up" in her family's stockade for nearly a year, and other accounts tell of Indian raids on livestock and occasional harm to settlers. The United States finally signed treaties allowing these Seminole and Miccosukee Indians living in the Everglades to remain in Florida on new reservations established for them in the area near Lake Okeechobee and the Everglades.

Orange County's vast territory forced judges, politicians, and anyone doing business with the county government to travel great distances to the centrally located county seat. The legislature responded to popular agitation by forming new counties from territory once part of Orange County. People living in the extreme southern part of Mosquito County petitioned for and won the creation of St. Lucie County in 1844. Residents east of the St.

Johns River secured the establishment of Volusia County in 1854. Brevard County became a separate entity in 1855.

The formation of the new counties reduced Orange County's size, and Mellonville, the county seat since 1845, no longer occupied a central location within the smaller county. In an election in 1856, Orange County voters selected the settlement near Fort Gatlin to be the new county seat. But the population had spread northward away from the Jernigan settlement and toward Lake Eola, leaving in question the exact site of the county seat. Land speculator Benjamin Caldwell resolved the dilemma when he deeded four acres of land near Lake Eola to the county for a courthouse. In 1857 the post office at Jernigan, near Fort Gatlin, closed and a new post office opened at Lake Eola in the new town of Orlando.

The population in Central Florida remained scattered, averaging fewer than two people per square mile during the first two decades, from 1845 to 1865. Several families homesteaded the Fort Christmas area in the 1850s and 1860s. Colonel Isaac Hudson and Judge James G. Speer bought land south of Lake Apopka, now the town of Oakland, in the 1850s. R.C. Roper purchased land in the vicinity of Winter Garden in 1859. Homesteaders relied chiefly on subsistence farming, hogs, and cattle. The well-drained soil, slightly rolling surface, and healthy climate around Lake Apopka supported cotton, sugar cane, and sweet potatoes. Large herds of range cattle grazed on vast prairies of mostly poorly drained flatwoods extending south to Kissimmee and east to Fort Christmas. Some settlers planted small orange groves and some occasionally had surplus sugar cane to sell. Some tapped the abundant pine trees for turpentine and pitch. Deer skins and the pelts of otter and other fur-bearing animals provided cash for necessities settlers could not grow, and for those who planted cotton, the long staple variety grew well and brought excellent prices.

Though the cattle industry dominated Central Florida's economy and way of life, Florida was a cotton producing state and a slave state. In 1860, just before the start of the Civil War, Florida's African-American slaves numbered 61,745, more than forty percent of the total state population. More than half of the slaves lived and worked in six plantation counties near the Georgia border. The only cotton plantations in Orange County large enough to rely on slave labor were in the vicinity of Lakes Monroe and Apopka, but a few farmers and cattlemen used slave labor, and some Central Florida households included slaves.

Aaron Jernigan brought African Americans to Central Florida in 1842 to tend his cattle. In 1850 Major Starke worked fifteen hands in his Orange County sugar cane fields. Jacob Summerlin traded slaves for cattle to establish his herd, as did Samuel Hudson. In 1850 Orange County included Volusia and Brevard Counties, and 226 slaves made up forty-eight

Above: Fugitive slaves became part of the Seminole tribe and are still known as "Black Seminoles."

COURTESY OF THE STATE ARCHIVES OF FLORIDA

Below: John Horse was a Black Seminole chief of African, Indian, and Spanish ancestry who served as Coacoochee's interpreter. During the Second Seminole War, Osceola and Chief Alligator often consulted with him about their strategies.

COURTESY OF THE STATE ARCHIVES OF FLORIDA

percent of the total population of 466. In 1860, with Volusia and Brevard counties gone, slaves accounted for sixteen percent of Orange County's population of 987. At the start of the Civil War 29 owners held a total of 163 slaves: 14 in Orlando, 43 in Mellonville (now Sanford), 7 in Hawkinsville (on the St. Johns River), and 99 in District 3 (Apopka, Wekiva, and Winter Garden).

Abraham Lincoln was elected president of the United States in 1860, and on January 10, 1861, Florida seceded from the Union. Central Florida, still sparsely settled and with few slaves, had little interest in secession or war. Orange County's representative at the Secession Convention, William Woodruff, cast one of only seven votes against secession. Central Florida men joined the Confederate Army, but most fought far from home. Florida's only major Civil War battles took place in northern Florida at Olustee and Natural Bridge.

Throughout the Confederacy life was hard for the women left behind to care for families, farms, and businesses while husbands and fathers served with the army. Supplies went to the army, and like the rest of the South, Orange County suffered from shortages of food and other provisions. Cattlemen, though, especially Central Florida's Jacob Summerlin, prospered during the war, supplying beef for the Confederate Army. Florida's other important wartime commodity came from the salt works along the coasts. The Union blockade deprived the South of salt, necessary for preserving meat as well as for seasoning food. Commercial salt works provided for the army, but individual Floridians traveled to the coast to make salt from sea water for their own use.

Orange County's population grew during the Civil War as people moved further south to escape the fighting. The growth continued after the war ended. Southerners displaced by the war, and others drawn by orange groves and balmy temperatures, moved to Florida. Citrus fruit came to Florida with the first Spanish explorers, and the earliest settlers found the trees growing wild. Growers grafted sweeter varieties to the hardy but sour pioneer trees to establish profitable groves and launch the citrus industry. The first groves operated near Lake Monroe because the fruit was shipped north by steamboat, but with the arrival of the railroad commercial citrus production moved south into what is now Orange County.

Turpentine became Florida's second largest industry after citrus. Florida's pine forests yielded naval stores for European ships in the mid-1500s, and by 1850 small turpentine camps in Florida produced one-fourth of U.S.

Orange County's 1857 Revenue records include the values of all slaves held within the county.

COURTESY OF THE ORANGE COUNTY REGIONAL HISTORY CENTER.

naval stores. In 1900 Florida's naval stores industry had a value of $8 million. A turpentine camp in East Orange County in the 1870s became Curryville, now in Seminole County. Other camps at Snow Hill and on Fort Christmas Road have also become part of Seminole County. Orange County's turpentine industry, which lasted into the 1930s, also operated in the pine woods near Apopka, Ocoee, Lake Mary, Longwood, and the less-settled areas south of Orlando.

Settlers came despite the lack of passable roads into what remained mostly unsettled frontier and despite Orlando's reputation as a wide-open, cattle town. Cow herders stole cattle, altered brands, and fought with each other. Bone Mizell was said to have ridden his cow pony into an Orange Avenue saloon. In 1868, on the night before an important cattle rustling trial, arsonists set fire to the two-story log county courthouse. It burned to the ground, and with it went not only the records of the case to be tried, but also nearly all county records prior to that time. The lawlessness climaxed in 1870, with the murder of Orange County Sheriff David Mizell, who was ambushed on his way to collect a cattle tax from a prominent rancher. The ensuing feud between two cattle families took the lives of several men and drove others into flight to Texas.

The difficulty of getting into the interior of Central Florida probably slowed Orange County's growth more than any other factor.

Above: Florida's cattle are distant relatives of Texas Longhorn cattle.

COURTESY OF THE ORANGE COUNTY REGIONAL HISTORY CENTER.

Bottom, left: Jacob Summerlin supplied the Confederate Army with beef during the Civil War.

COURTESY OF THE ORANGE COUNTY REGIONAL HISTORY CENTER.

Bottom, right: Cotton was big industry in Florida prior to the Civil War.

COURTESY OF THE STATE ARCHIVES OF FLORIDA.

People and supplies made the difficult and sometimes uncertain journey up the St. Johns River by steamboat, across Lake Monroe to Sanford, and then overland to Orlando, often by ox cart. Nonetheless, Orange County's population, 2,195 in 1870, increased to 6,618 in 1880. It nearly doubled during the 1880s, to 12,584 in 1890, despite the loss of territory in 1887 to create Lake and Osceola Counties. Orlando, the seat of Orange County government, incorporated in 1875, though it remained a village of about eighty-five people. Apopka, Maitland, Oakland, and Winter Park incorporated during 1880s.

In 1880 the South Florida Railroad began laying tracks from Sanford to Tampa, bringing an economic boom to Orange County. Cattle shipped to market by rail arrived in better condition, and citrus fruit reached northern markets while still fresh. Citrus quickly became more important than cotton or sugar cane, and growers planted more trees. Property values, especially orange groves, increased during the 1880s. The railroad made travel easier for everyone, and businesses appeared and hotels opened to accommodate the first wave of tourists. The South Florida Railroad, renamed the Atlantic Coast Line in 1902, brought boom times to Orlando, while the Florida Midland Railroad and the Orange Belt Railway benefitted communities in western Orange County.

Advertisements in London newspapers in the 1880s attracted English immigrants to Central Florida, where the ideal climate and developing citrus industry promised a comfortable future. Known as the English Colony, these British settlers bought large tracts of land around Orlando, where they planted citrus groves and played polo. Freezing weather in the winter of 1894-1895 ended Central Florida's first economic boom and sent many of the English growers home to England. Florida had survived serious freezes in 1836 and 1885, and cold weather frequently damaged citrus crops, but that winter successive hard freezes destroyed the groves. The first, in December 1894, killed the fruit on the trees. Then in February 1895, a second freeze killed the trees, many to the ground. Forced to start all over again, growers gave up and left Florida. Many of the Englishmen abandoned their properties. Eight out of ten banks closed their doors, and the population fell to 11,374 in 1900. The citrus industry took fifteen years to recover. Growers who stayed bought groves cheaply in a glutted market. Some smaller growers survived, but the era of giant groves began with the devastating freezes.

In 1910 Orange County led Florida's citrus producers. The citrus industry concentrated in the western Orange County communities of Apopka, Ocoee, Orlando, Tildenville, Windermere, and Winter Garden. By 1920, Orange County shipped one-fourth of the state's $20 million orange crop. Growers near

Above: David Mizell was Orange County's first sheriff.

COURTESY OF THE ORANGE COUNTY REGIONAL HISTORY CENTER.

Below: Cattle were free to roam throughout Florida until the fence law was enacted in 1949.

COURTESY OF THE ORANGE COUNTY REGIONAL HISTORY CENTER.

Sanford and Oviedo, then in northeastern Orange County, turned to celery and other vegetable crops after the freeze killed the citrus trees in 1895, and commercial vegetable growers predominated in 1913 when that part of Orange County separated to become Seminole County, with Sanford as its county seat. With that final cession of territory to create another county, Orange County's original 7,000 square miles became approximately 1,000 square miles. Winter Garden incorporated in 1908 and Taft in 1912.

The automobile changed Central Florida in the 1920s as it changed the rest of the country. Automobile owners demanded good roads, and the new roads, particularly the Dixie Highway, completed from Canada to Miami in 1925, brought people to Florida. More and more tourists arrived by automobile rather than by train, and many stayed to live in Florida. The Great Florida Land Boom followed as everyone tried to invest in real estate. Land sold and resold at ever-higher prices, and housing developments multiplied. Banks, realtors, and construction companies prospered. The frenzy finally ended when prices went too high and hurricanes in South Florida in 1926 and 1928 warned off would-be residents. The resulting slump pushed Florida into the Great Depression ahead of the rest of the country.

The Cheney Highway, completed in 1924, linked Orange County with Florida's eastern coast and prolonged the land boom in Central Florida. Builders laid out new subdivisions throughout the county, more than thirty in Winter Park alone. The value of building permits in Orlando grew from $1.8 million in 1920 to $8.6 million in 1926. The county population increased by almost two and one half times from 19,890 in 1920 to 49,737 in 1930. Belle Isle, Bithlo, Edgewood, and Orlo Vista incorporated, and Winter Park and Winter Garden re-incorporated as cities in the 1920s. The county school system consolidated and improved its buildings. Orange County grew to 70,074 people by 1940, despite the economic slowdown of the Great Depression.

Citrus remained the largest and most important crop in a primarily agricultural economy into the 1940s. Agricultural productivity helped determine land values, with grazing land selling for as little as twenty-five cents an acre in the 1930s. But pastureland also made good airfields, and Central Florida's ideal flying weather attracted pilots and commercial airlines. Orange

Above: A devastated orange grove after the 1895 freeze.

COURTESY OF THE ORANGE COUNTY REGIONAL HISTORY CENTER.

Below: Construction of I-4 between Orlando and Winter Park, April 10, 1959.

COURTESY OF THE ORANGE COUNTY REGIONAL HISTORY CENTER.

Above: The Orlando Air Base is only one highlight in Orange County's aviation history.

COURTESY OF THE ORANGE COUNTY REGIONAL HISTORY CENTER.

Below: NATO representatives visited the Martin Orlando (now Lockheed Martin) plant in the 1950s.

COURTESY OF THE ORANGE COUNTY REGIONAL HISTORY CENTER.

County's first airport, Buck Field, opened in 1922, and Orlando Municipal Airport followed in 1928. Municipal Airport became the Orlando Army Air Field in December 1940 when the United States began preparations for World War II. The Army developed strategic bombing tactics at a second air base, the Pine Castle Army Air Field, which opened in Orange County south of Orlando in 1942. The bases brought thousands of servicemen to the area for training during World War II, and many returned to live in Orange County when the war ended.

Road building stimulated growth in Orange County after the war. Highway 50, completed in 1949, spread development to rural areas, such as Pine Hills to the west of Orlando. By the mid-1950s, traffic problems on Highway 441, the Orange Blossom Trail,

necessitated a widening project. Both Florida's Turnpike and Interstate 4 began construction during the 1950s. Good highways, two military bases, a potential civilian work force, and abundant water supplies, brought the Glenn L. Martin Company to Orange County in 1956. The Martin Company aircraft defense plant south of Orlando affected not only the county economy, but also property values as well. As the population grew, land use in Orange County shifted from agricultural to urban.

Still, the citrus industry continued to drive the economy through the 1970s. Of the four major citrus producing regions in Florida, the Upper Interior, which includes Orange County, produced 40 percent of Florida's crop in 1957, however a series of freezing years in the 1980s wiped out a century of cultivated groves. Citrus production moved further south, and the Upper Interior district production fell to 6 percent of the total. Housing developments replaced the orange groves.

The establishment of Cape Canaveral in Brevard County in 1950 brought the space program to Central Florida, and community leaders increased their efforts to promote Orange County. In order to accommodate the new jet passenger planes, Orlando leaders negotiated an arrangement to share a jet runway at McCoy Air Force Base in 1962. Promoters succeeded in changing the route of the Sunshine Parkway, to bring it through Orange County and past the Martin Company plant. The north-south Sunshine Parkway, completed in 1963 and later renamed Florida's Turnpike, put Orange County in a bargaining position for routing of Interstate 4, the northeast-southwest highway connecting Tampa and Daytona Beach. Interstate 4 opened in 1965, and in 1967 the Martin Andersen Beeline linked Orlando's airport with the Cape Canaveral area.

Florida Technological University opened in Orange County in 1968. Ten years later the name changed to University of Central Florida. Valencia Community College opened on its own campus in 1971. As the air force reduced its use of the Orlando Air Force Base, county promoters secured another military

Top: Splash Mountain is one of the most popular rides at The Magic Kingdom inside Walt Disney World.

PHOTO BY MICHAEL LOWIN

Middle: The lighthouse tower at Universal Orlando's Islands of Adventure theme park.

PHOTO BY DAVID BJORGEN

Bottom: Orca whales perform at SeaWorld of Orlando.

PHOTO BY DAVID BJORGEN

installation to replace it, and the first seamen entered the Orlando Naval Training Center in 1968.

Walt Disney selected Orange County, with its year round vacation weather and easy access to good transportation for his new amusement park. Only a few people knew the identity of the company that bought twenty-seven thousand acres in southern Orange and northern Osceola Counties, until November 15, 1965, when Walt and Roy Disney announced that they would build an entertainment complex. Walt Disney World opened in 1971. Other theme parks followed, creating an unprecedented economic boom. Sea World opened in 1973, and Wet 'n Wild in 1977. Existing parks added rides and attractions with something new opening nearly every year. Disney opened EPCOT Center in 1982, MGM Studios in 1989, and Animal Kingdom in 1998. Universal Studios opened a movie-themed park in 1990, and followed that with expansions, including Islands of Adventure in 1999. Tourism expanded dramatically; hotels, restaurants, and gas stations multiplied. The former grove land became housing for Orange County's growing population, which reached 896,344 in 2000.

For more than one hundred years Orange County operated under a system of government established by the state constitution in 1881 for rural, frontier Florida. A county without a charter must adhere to the form of government prescribed for non-chartered cities and can change its form of government only by adopting a charter. Orange County voters approved the first charter in 1986. In 1988 voters decided to change from at-large elections to single-member district elections, to add a sixth commissioner, and to elect the county chairman rather than allowing commissioners to choose a chairman. The Orange County Charter requires that a review commission meet every four years to study the county government and place proposed changes on the ballot. In 2004 voters approved changing the charter to give the position of the county chairman to the Orange County mayor.

Orange County entered the twenty-first century with a total population of 896,344, an increase of 32 percent over 1990. Caucasians represented 68.6 percent of the total, with Hispanics or Latinos second with 18.8 percent. African Americans accounted for 18.2 percent in 2000, and Asians 3.4 percent. In 2002, statistics showed that the county had moved almost completely from rural to urban in its less than two centuries of existence. The rural population made up only ten percent of the total in 2002, with ninety percent of Orange County residents living in urban places. By 2005, fewer than ten thousand acres remained in citrus groves.

The Orange County Convention Center is the second largest convention center in the United States with seven million square feet of total space.

PHOTO BY NEHRAMS2020

Apopka

BY CYNTHIA CARDONA MELÉNDEZ

What do sweet potatoes and ferns have in common? Nothing, unless you are the city of Apopka, Florida. Located in Northwest Orange County, Apopka's proximity to Wekiwa Springs and Lake Apopka, the second largest lake in Florida, was of major importance to its development, making the area an ideal trading center for Orange County by the 1850s. The town's strategic location also made it a transportation hub for Central Florida since goods for the area were transported by barge via the St. Johns and Wekiwa Rivers to Wekiwa Springs. Apopka was originally called "The Lodge" since its central location was naturally a good spot for the first Masonic lodge in Orange County, founded in 1856. Once the city was chartered in 1882, it was given the name Apopka City which was then shortened to Apopka. The name Apopka was derived from Lake Apopka, and is an Indian word meaning "big potato" due to the large crops of sweet potatoes grown by the area's original Native American inhabitants.

By the early 1900s, Apopka's valuable location near Lake Apopka allowed the city to flourish in numerous ways. The lake's thirty-five miles of shoreline afforded Apopka the opportunity to grow enough

Miss Apopka and Miss Lake Apopka 1951 pose for a Central Florida Fair promotional shot.

COURTESY OF THE ORANGE COUNTY REGIONAL HISTORY CENTER

citrus and vegetables to constitute the creation of the Apopka Board of Trade, which acted as an advocate for the construction of a railway near Apopka in order to give the town access to markets outside of the state. The opening of the Florida Railway and Navigation Company made this dream a reality, and, soon after, the push for and the eventual construction of good, passable roads also allowed for greater industry in Apopka.

In the 1920s, small acres of ferns grown by small landowners Harry Ustler and Walter Newell eventually became a substantial part of Apopka's economy. Fern growers first grew

Above: The Seaboard Air Line Railroad was in operation from the 1880s until 1967 when it merged with the Atlantic Coast Line Railroad to form the Seaboard Coast Line Railroad. The Apopka Depot was built in 1900 and was placed on the National Register of Historic Places in 1993.

PHOTO BY JOHN BRADLEY.

Right: The William Edwards Hotel was named for an Apopka pioneer of the same name. In 1926, the residents of Apopka formed a corporation and sold bonds to build the $180,000 hotel. The building was razed in 1963.

COURTESY OF THE ORANGE COUNTY REGIONAL HISTORY CENTER.

Below: Residents of Apopka gathered together in June 1911 for a community barbeque.

COURTESY OF THE ORANGE COUNTY REGIONAL HISTORY CENTER.

Boston ferns on small plots of land less than an acre in size but, by mid-decade, the industry expanded to include many types of ferns on large acreage. In 1924, Apopka adopted the slogan "Fern City," and the Apopka Chamber of Commerce initiated a marketing campaign describing Apopka as the "heart of Summerland where all the time is summer and the flowers never die" and as the city where " two acres in ferns is sufficient to afford the industrious grower a livelihood." By 1930, over a million ferns were being shipped out of Apopka with Orlando department stores as the largest buyer. That same year, the Orange County Fern Clearing House Association was created and headquartered in Apopka. The Association controlled 95 percent of fern production in the area, employing nearly 500 people during the shipping season and selling nearly $500,000 worth of ferns by the mid-1930s. Apopka moved beyond just ferns and in 1965 changed its slogan to "Indoor Foliage Capitol of the World" to better encompass its expanding business in tropical foliage, cut flowers, blooming plants, roses, and bulbs. By 1968, Apopka grew two thirds of the foliage in the state of Florida, bringing $8 million to the state's economy.

Since 1949, Apopka has been led by Mayor John Land. Land has served as mayor of Apopka for fifty-six years, making him, at eighty-eight years old, the longest serving mayor in Florida. After returning from service in the army in World War II, Land became mayor of Apopka at the age of twenty-nine and served uncontested until 1967. That year, Land was defeated by an Apopka city commissioner. Land concentrated on his bulk oil business and ran in the next mayoral election, becoming mayor again in 1970 and remaining in office until today.

Mayor Land and the City of Apopka received national attention in 2001 when the Apopka Little League defeated a team from Bronx, New York, to win the United States Little League World Series, bringing a sense of tremendous pride to the "Fern City."

Above: Standish Lake, located on the Pirie (later Errol) Estate, was a popular location for leisurely horse and buggy rides.

COURTESY OF THE ORANGE COUNTY REGIONAL HISTORY CENTER.

Below: John T. Pirie, chairman of the board of the Chicago department store Carson Pirie Scott & Co., owned a winter home in Apopka. He hired local resident William Edwards to manage the estate. Pirie's home and garden, shown here, were razed in 1971.

COURTESY OF THE ORANGE COUNTY REGIONAL HISTORY CENTER

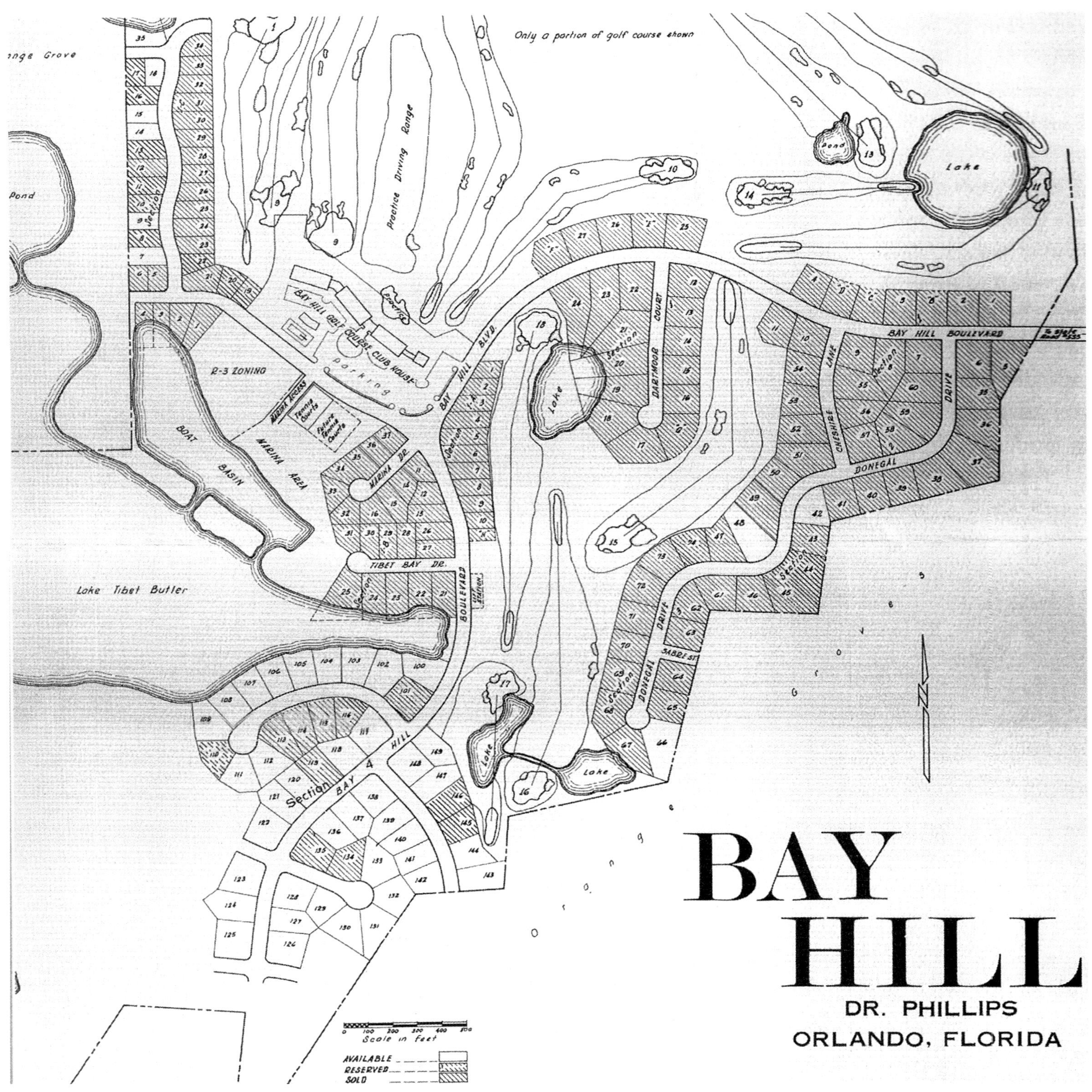

A map of the Bay Hill Community showing a portion of the golf course.

COURTESY OF THE ORANGE COUNTY REGIONAL HISTORY CENTER.

Bay Hill

BY STEPHANIE GAUB

Going green is not new to Orange County. Dr. Phillip Phillips, the original owner of what is now Bay Hill, pioneered local environmental awareness during the 1950s when he made provisions for his vast acreage in southwest Orange County. From the 1920s to the 1950s, Dr. Phillips owned and operated the world's largest citrus processing center located ten miles south and west of the city of Orlando and, by 1950, was the largest land owner in Orange County. He owned so much land that that part of the county was referred to as "Dr. Phillips, Florida." In 1954, he sold all of his citrus groves but kept his uncultivated land. This "raw" land became the community of Bay Hill.

In the 1940s, Dr. Phillips prepared a plan for his non-citrus-bearing land. Completed at a time when Orange County did not have comprehensive zoning regulations, he created planning initiatives to minimize the environmental impact of future land development, including the construction of water retention basins.

In the late 1950s, the PGA of America wanted to move its headquarters from Dunedin, Florida. Upon hearing this, local civic-minded individuals tried to bring the organization to Orlando. Howard Phillips, son of Dr. Phillips and President of the Dr. Phillips Foundation, suggested a 640-acre tract of land owned by the Foundation west of Apopka-Vineland Road. The land did not appeal to the PGA but piqued the interest of Tommy Barnes. In 1959, Barnes partnered with a group of businessmen in Nashville, Tennessee and, by June 14, 1960, the Bay Hill Club, Inc., formed. Pursuant to Dr. Phillips' environmental regulations, the Club maintained the golf course as a greenbelt area to protect the Butler Chain of Lakes.

Stipulations required the Bay Hill Club, Inc., to build a permanent entrance road with housing developments on either side. While Tommy Barnes dreamed of a world-class golf club, Dr. Phillips and his son dreamed of a first-class residential development that could serve as a model for future growth while preserving open green space.

Despite numerous efforts by Bay Hill's investors, people seemed more interested in obtaining a membership to the Bay Hill Club & Lodge rather than placing their stakes in real estate. Once Walt Disney announced his plans to build a theme park nearby, significant improvements, including the construction of a second lodge building and an additional nine-hole course, Bay Hill experienced a modest increase in lot sales and home construction. However, despite these enhancements, people still thought of the area as "out in the boondocks, next to nothing," and "simply, a jungle."

Arnold Palmer purchased the Club in 1976 and upgraded the golf course to meet PGA standards. As a result, Bay Hill hosts the annual Arnold Palmer Invitational which has been won by luminaries such as Ernie Els, Vijay Singh, and Tiger Woods. The Bay Hill community is home to some of Orlando's most affluent residents. From humble beginnings to the home of a major professional golf tournament, Bay Hill has maintained the original vision of Dr. Phillips as an exemplary environmentally conscious Orange County community.

STATE OF FLORIDA
ORANGE COUNTY } SS.

I, J. Clement Brossier, Gen. Mgr.

of the REPORTER-STAR, a newspaper printed and published at Orlando, State and County aforesaid, do solemnly swear that an advertisement, a true copy of which is hereunto affixed, was published in said REPORTER-STAR, once a week for three consecutive weeks from the 21st day of May to 4th day of June A. D., 1924, inclusive.

J. Clement Brossier

Subscribed and sworn to before me this 17th day of June A. D., 1924.

C. W. S. Stowe,
Notary Public

Publication Fee, $9.20

NOTICE TO CONTRACTORS

NOTICE IS HEREBY GIVEN that at 3 P. M., on the 12th day of June, A. D. 1924, the City Council of the Town of Bithlo, Florida, will sit in the City Hall of said Town of Bithlo to open bids for contracts in connection with the grading, paving and hard-surfacing of the following streets in said Town within the following limits:

Seventh Street from Eleventh Ave. to Adams Ave.;
Eighth Street from Fifth Ave. to Third Ave.;
Sixth Street from Sixth Ave. to Washington Ave.;
Fifth Street from Eleventh Ave. to Fifth Ave.;
Sixth Avenue from Sixth St. to Seventh St.;
Fifth Avenue F. E. C. to Seventh St.;
Fifth Avenue from Seventh St. to Ninth St.;

and to award such contract. Contract to be awarded subject to the satisfactory sale of bonds. Work to be done in accordance with the plans and specifications now on file in the office of the City Clerk of the Town of Bithlo and the Contractor to agree to furnish bond satisfactory to the City Council and to enter into a contract to be approved by the City's Attorneys.

This 24th day of March, A. D. 1924.

S. P. BAILEY,
President, City Council of Town of Bithlo, Florida.

ATTEST:
M. M. Macey,
City Clerk, Town of Bithlo, Florida.

APPROVED:
J. R. Parker,
Mayor, Town of Bithlo, Florida.

5—21-28—6-4—

In the 1920s, Bithlo worked hard to improve its streets.

COURTESY OF THE ORANGE COUNTY REGIONAL HISTORY CENTER.

BITHLO

BY GARRET KREMER-WRIGHT

The "Gateway to Orange County" or Bithlo was established in 1912. Henry Flagler's wife named the town after the Seminole word meaning either "outlook" or "canoe." It was one of a handful of communities that sprang up alongside the Florida East Coast Railway's Okeechobee Branch.

Bithlo flourished in its early days of existence. Several lumber companies set up operations in 1915. These included Rutherford and Osceola Lumber Companies along with Brown and McIntosh mills. In 1920 Pocataw Lumber was added to the ranks. These companies fed off the heavy stands of pine and cypress trees that surrounded the town. In 1918, a school was established. Bithlo was laid out in 1920 by Bailey and Scott. Their plan included five miles of paved streets. The town had seven dwellings by 1922, which allowed the city to become incorporated. The opening of the Cheney-Dixie Highway in December 1924 allowed the city to undertake the necessary improvements to make the town a viable place to live.

In 1924, the town voted to issue an $80,000 bond for internal improvements. These improvements included electric lights, water plants, and paved roads. The investors hoped that this would help to draw people to the community, but unfortunately only seven additional buildings were erected by 1926.

After 1926, the prosperity that began in 1920 began to take a downward spiral. Far from a population center, Bithlo never really had a chance at expansion. This along with the collapse of the Florida land boom caused the town to default on its loans. This led to the town's rapid decline. The decline began with the school's closure in 1929. The Great Depression of the 1930s further hampered Bithlo. By 1941, town council meetings ceased, and the Okeechobee Railroad Branch was abandoned in 1944. The Bithlo Livestock Market tried to bring the town back to life in 1950 but was only able to stay afloat until 1954. After World War II the town was seen as a waste dumping and pollution site, which left much of the town in a state of disrepair. In 1970, residents petitioned the state legislature to revoke their town's charter. The town was unincorporated in 1977. However, one problem remained: the lawsuit brought on by a group of Miami investors. These investors bought half the town's interest on the bonds issued in 1924 and now wanted payment for the debt that totaled $300,000 by 1982. The courts ruled that the residents of Biltho did not have to pay the money back.

With that final legal issue solved, Biltho was able to get back to being the small town it always had been. There is relatively little there today as far as businesses are concerned, and Bithlo is just another small community that has been swallowed up by the ever-widening Orlando metropolitan area.

CHRISTMAS

BY STEPHANIE GAUB

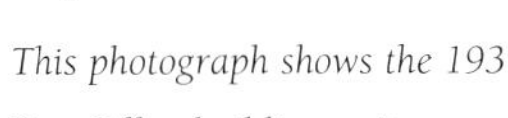

This photograph shows the 1937 Christmas Post Office building as it appeared in 1950.
COURTESY OF THE ORANGE COUNTY REGIONAL HISTORY CENTER.

Every holiday season thousands of people flock to the Christmas, Florida, post office to have their cards and packages stamped with the Christmas postmark. Out-of-towners also send bundles of mail to the post office just so it can receive the special Christmas cancellation. At this time of year, the sleepy little town of just over eleven hundred leaps into the national spotlight. All of this makes it hard to imagine that the town that boasts a Christmas tree all year round once housed a fort built during the Second Seminole War to protect United States troops.

The Second Seminole War began on December 23, 1835, when a party of 111 officers and enlisted men left Fort Brooke (now Tampa, Florida) to bring reinforcements to Fort King (now Ocala, Florida). A group of Seminoles ambushed the men and all but three were killed in a battle known today as Dade's Massacre. In an effort to help white settlers battle the Seminole Indians, the United States built several forts throughout Florida. In his diary dated December 27, 1837, Surgeon N. S. Jarvis states, "Today we finished our Fort which we called Fort Christmas having commenced it on that day." Lieutenant W. B. Davis described the fort as "...80 feet square of pine pickets with two substantial block houses 20 feet square...." After the troops left Fort Christmas on January 3, 1838, the area remained mostly unpopulated for over a decade.

In 1842 the United States government established the Armed Occupation and Settlement Act to encourage settlement in Florida. The act gave settlers 160 acres of land to Florida residents provided that they did not already own at least 160 acres, resided on the land for at least five years after obtaining it, cultivated at least five acres of land during the first year, and built a house on the lot within the first year. John Richard A. Tucker, Albert Roberts, Andrew Jackson Barber, William Jackson Osteen, Samuel and Henry Hodges, John W. Tanner, and Marion Canada were among the first to take

advantage of settling the Christmas area. These early settlers planted citrus groves and raised cattle and hogs.

The Tucker family became one of the most prominent Christmas families, and it seems as if ranching and working at the post office ran in the family's bloodstream. J. R. A. Tucker established a ranch in the 1860s on over sis hundred acres of land, and his grandson, Cecil A. Tucker, I, continued the family business. The younger Tucker also helped establish the Central Florida Cattlemen's Association in the early 1900s. Cecil's wife, Juanita, served as postmistress for forty-two years, succeeding her mother-in-law, who held the position for sixteen years. Cecil passed away in 1994 at the age of eighty-six and Juanita passed away in 2008 at the age of 101. The next generation of Tuckers continues to run the ranch, maintaining the family's strong ties to Christmas' agricultural heritage.

Christmas native Hughlette "Tex" Wheeler's work can be seen by visitors to Santa Anita racetrack in Arcadia, California, every time they pass the life-size statue of the great thoroughbred Seabiscuit. Wheeler created many famous works, including a statue of Will Rogers and his horse Soapsuds that is on display at the Will Rogers Museum in Claremore, Oklahoma. In 1998 the Fort Christmas Historical Society obtained six of Wheeler's sculptures that his family had recast from the original molds. Orange County Commissioners allocated monies for the purchase of the reproductions, and they can be seen at the Fort Christmas Historical Park Museum through its "Arts in the Parks" project.

Residents of Christmas remain proud of the town's heritage and close-knit community ties. Through its involvement in the Second Seminole Wars to the accomplishments of its residents, Christmas, Florida, continues to leave its mark on the history of Central Florida as well as the nation.

Top, left: A replica of the original Fort Christmas was constructed in 1976 and is operated by Orange County Parks and Recreation.

COURTESY OF THE STATE ARCHIVES OF FLORIDA

Above: Children pose in front of the year-round Christmas tree in Christmas, Florida, circa 1950.

COURTESY OF THE ORANGE COUNTY REGIONAL HISTORY CENTER

Below: Christmas, Florida, native Hughlette "Tex" Wheeler sculpted this statue of Seabiscuit.

COURTESY OF THE ORANGE COUNTY REGIONAL HISTORY CENTER

CONWAY

BY BARBARA KNOWLES

Reverend Charles William Arnold moved to Conway from England in 1885 and built Arnold's Court. In addition to his home, he added a private chapel and a ten-room barracks for other young Englishmen in need of housing.

COURTESY OF THE ORANGE COUNTY REGIONAL HISTORY CENTER

Located seven miles southeast of Orlando, Conway has been a community of diversity where at one time, the unmistakable crack of a cowman's whip might be heard not far from the aristocratic accent of an Englishman asking, "Polo, anyone?" Pioneers began homesteading the area, originally called Prospect, in the early 1870s by planting, for the most part, orange groves on the shores of Lake Conway. The epicenter of the settlement in 1874 was a log cabin at the crossroads of what is now Conway and Anderson roads. The structure served as a church, school, and all-purpose meeting space for residents.

Except for small areas of development, Central Florida's vast wilderness was home to cowmen who knew no fences or political boundaries. Prior to the Civil War, Moses Barber amassed a fortune in cattle in Northern Florida, but by the war's end, his fortune had dwindled. He moved his family south of the Conway settlement where he became a rival rancher with another prominent family, the Mizells. Competing for the same range caused friction among the groups, and their feud erupted when David Mizell, Orange County's first sheriff, was assassinated February 21, 1870. A series of incidences provoked the Barbers, and when the sheriff rode into Barber territory trying to collect a debt for a rancher, he was shot and killed. By the time the feud ended three months later, at least nine people were dead, one on the shore of Lake Conway.

Less than twenty years after the infamous Barber-Mizell feud, a group of Englishmen moved to Conway as the result of an aggressive advertising campaign in their country promoting Florida's opportunities. Known as the English Colony, their lifestyle contrasted sharply with that of the town's ordinary citizens, yet they brought culture that enriched the area. Three socioeconomic classes made up the colony, an older group of retired professional men and army officers seeking a mild climate, and a younger group, sons of gentlemen supported by remittances from home. The third class consisted of laborers who came as servants for the first two groups.

Most of the Englishmen favored sport over employment. After organizing a yacht club, they held regattas on Lake Conway and made hunting for small game such as quail and pigeons part of their activities. In 1888 they started playing polo using cow ponies on a field where Dover Shores Shopping Center is today. Two years later, they organized into the Orlando Polo Club and played against teams from all over the United States. Matches were social occasions with parades before the contests and tea served at the break periods between chukkers. The majority of the English Colony left Conway after the devastating citrus freezes of 1894 and 1895.

Nearly one hundred years later, another devastating freeze changed Conway forever. Once the cowmen and Englishmen left, large citrus groves consumed the area until the mid-1980s when back to back tree-destroying freezes forced growers to sell their land for real estate development. Today, Conway has become a large suburb of Orlando.

Polo was very popular among Conway's English settlers.

COURTESY OF THE ORANGE COUNTY REGIONAL HISTORY CENTER.

Dr. Phillips

BY TANA MOSIER PORTER

The Dr. Phillips Company's Sand Lake Packing Plant as seen from the air, c. 1940.

COURTESY OF THE ORANGE COUNTY REGIONAL HISTORY CENTER

The community of Dr. Phillips on the Butler Chain of Lakes in Southwest Orange County took its name from the citrus giant whose former groves it occupies. But the town owes much more than its name and location to Dr. Philip Phillips. Dr. Phillips bought acreage in Orange County and planted citrus groves beginning around 1900, and eventually became the largest individual citrus grove owner in the world. In 1917, Dr. Phillips envisioned a planned community on an 324-square-mile property he owned on the Butler lakes. In 1928, some grove workers lived near the Dr. Phillips Company Grove in houses Dr. Phillips provided. Dr. Phillips housed other workers in the Quarters, also part of the Dr. Phillips community. The children attended the one-room school at nearby Zantee, now Bay Hill.

During the late 1940s, Dr. Phillips followed through with his original community idea. He had a master land use plan drawn for an agricultural village of about 5,000 people. The community would be self-sustaining because the residents would work in his citrus groves, citrus packing house, and citrus fertilizer plant. In 1954, Dr. Phillips sold his citrus operation to the Minute Maid Company and went out of the citrus business. Before he died in 1959, Dr. Phillips considered replacing the emphasis on citrus employees with a plan that would encourage residential and industrial development.

In the early 1960s, Dr. Phillips, Inc., revised the master plan to provide for the Bay Hill Club and Bay Hill subdivision. The company created a new and more comprehensive plan in 1969, as Walt

Disney World neared completion just to the south of Dr. Phillips. The new land use plan could accommodate a community of fifty thousand residents, and The Marketplace, with shops and offices, would function as the community's downtown or commercial district. The 1969 plan became a reality after Disney World opened in 1971.

The original plan set aside land for schools. In 1979, Dr. Phillips, Inc., built the Dr. Phillips Elementary School because the area did not meet the state population requirement for a school. Dr. Phillips soon leased and then sold the school to the Orange County School System. The Dr. Phillips Company built and owns the Bay Hill Fire Station and leases it to the county. The Dr. Phillips Foundation owns the YMCA site and leases it to the Young Men's Christian Association. The Dr. Phillips Foundation designed and built the Southwest Library on Della Drive and leases it to the Orange County Library System. The Dr. Phillips Company built a water treatment plant for the town. Dr. Philip Phillips provided a cemetery on the Apopka-Vineland Road, where he and his wife, Della, are buried. Originally for grove employees, it now accepts all burials.

By the 1990s, Dr. Phillips had become one of Orange County's hottest growth locations, catering to an affluent population. Residents appreciated the planned land use and controlled growth, but annexations by Orlando remained a threat to the character of the community, and residents feared continuing encroachment from the Universal Studios Florida theme park. In 1998 residents voted to have Dr. Phillips declared historically significant and designated as an Urban Preservation Area, protected from loss of territory to annexation by other communities. The population of Dr. Phillips had grown to 9,548 in 2000, 84 percent white, 3 percent black, and 8 percent Hispanic.

Above: Dr. Philip Phillips.
COURTESY OF THE ORANGE COUNTY REGIONAL HISTORY CENTER.

Bottom, left: "Commander" was one of several brands under which the Dr. Phillips Company packaged citrus.
COURTESY OF THE ORANGE COUNTY REGIONAL HISTORY CENTER.

Below: Minute Maid purchased the Dr. Phillips Company's land holdings in 1954.
COURTESY OF THE ORANGE COUNTY REGIONAL HISTORY CENTER.

EATONVILLE

BY CYNTHIA CARDONA MELÉNDEZ

Covered porch with areas for relaxation at the Hungerford Normal School, c. 1930.

COURTESY OF THE ORANGE COUNTY REGIONAL HISTORY CENTER

Orange County has the unique distinction to have within its boundaries the town of Eatonville, the oldest incorporated African American municipality in the United States. Eatonville owes its existence to the resourcefulness and progressive thinking of twenty-seven African American residents of nearby Maitland. After the Civil War, newly freed slaves came to Florida from all over the South searching for work. In Maitland, many found employment clearing the land, working in construction, and packing in the area's citrus groves. As Maitland flourished, so did its African American residents with many of them eventually owning businesses and land. With this progression came the idea to incorporate the land one mile west of Maitland into a town strictly governed by African Americans.

Difficulties arose when no one would sell land to the Maitland residents for the purpose of incorporating it into an all black municipality. The land was eventually purchased from Maitland resident Josiah Eaton by Lewis Lawrence and deeded to Joseph Clark, one of the twenty-seven African American men proposing incorporation. On August 15, 1887, a vote was passed to incorporate 112 acres in order to create the municipality of Eatonville, named after Josiah Eaton. Of the more than one hundred black towns founded between 1865 and 1900, fewer than twelve remain today, with Eatonville being the oldest.

By 1889, Eatonville had its own newspaper, the *Eatonville Speaker*, and most significantly, the first and only school for African Americans in Central Florida. Russell and Mary Calhoun, former students of the Tuskegee Institute in Alabama, founded The Robert Hungerford Normal and Industrial School. The Calhoun's modeled Hungerford School after the Tuskegee Institute in order to provide academic and vocational training for Eatonville students. Once word spread of the school's success, African American students came to attend Hungerford from all over the Southeast. The land on which the school was built was donated by Edward and Anna Hungerford, winter residents of Maitland, in honor of their son Dr. Robert Hungerford. Hungerford treated African American children suffering from malaria in Louisiana, eventually contracting and dying of the disease himself. After sixty years of independent existence, the administration of the Hungerford School came under Orange County Public Schools in 1950.

Eatonville's most famous citizen was acclaimed writer, folklorist, and cultural anthropologist Zora Neale Hurston. Hurston was the daughter of Reverend John Hurston, Eatonville's third mayor. Zora writes in her autobiography, *Dust Tracks on a Road*, in 1942 that her childhood in Eatonville provided an example of black achievement and the impetus to achieve her goals. Hurston graduated from Barnard College in 1928 and soon after became associated with the some of the greats of the Harlem Renaissance such as Langston Hughes. Her most famous work, *Their Eyes Were Watching God*, published in 1937, finally brought her national recognition. For nineteen years, Eatonville has celebrated Hurston's legacy and her ties to the town with the Zora Neale Hurston Festival of the Arts and Humanities every January.

Above: Eatonville Town Hall. On August 15, 1887, Eatonville became the first incorporated all-black town in the United States.

PHOTO BY SYDNEY POORE.

Bottom, left: Joe Clark and an unidentified man stand on the steps of a building in Eatonville, Florida.

COURTESY OF THE ORANGE COUNTY REGIONAL HISTORY CENTER.

Below: Zora Neale Hurston glorified Eatonville in her writings as a place where black Americans could live independent of white society.

COURTESY OF THE ORANGE COUNTY REGIONAL HISTORY CENTER.

EDGEWOOD

BY TANA MOSIER PORTER

The Dixie Highway ran through Edgewood.

COURTESY OF THE ORANGE COUNTY REGIONAL HISTORY CENTER

Edgewood lies along Orange Avenue three miles south of downtown Orlando. Its first residents followed the South Florida Railroad into the area when it extended its tracks from Orlando to Tampa in 1881. Railroad people and other business interests settled along the tracks where they passed through the area of Lakes Conway, Gatlin, and Jennie Jewel. The Dixie Highway, now Orange Avenue, parallels the railroad, and its paving in 1916 opened the area to further industrial and residential development. The Florida Land Boom of the 1920s brought significant residential expansion, which aroused an interest in incorporating the community, but divisive family and business factions refused to incorporate as one town. As a result, the area divided into three separate towns, Edgewood, Belle Isle, and Pine Castle, and all three towns received municipal charters in 1924 or 1925. Edgewood's charter was dated April 24, 1924.

Soon after the boom ended in 1926, governments in all three towns stopped meeting. Edgewood's City Council has no record of meeting between 1925 and 1955.

Environmental issues and encroachment from Orlando, as well as fears of the loss of their inactive charters, inspired both Belle Isle and Edgewood to reorganize to protect their interests as towns. Edgewood presented its reactivated town charter to the state in 1969, the same year the community built a town hall. Edgewood became a city in 1973.

The Central Connector controversy dominated Edgewood throughout the 1980s. The Central Connector, a six-lane highway connecting downtown Orlando with the Orlando International Airport, would have sliced through the center of Edgewood. Part of the Orlando Orange County Expressway Authority's 1983 Long Range Plan, the road won approval despite protests from Edgewood that it would destroy businesses and homes and bring noise and air pollution. Edgewood fought the road for nearly ten years, in court and in the press. In 1994 the Expressway Authority finally removed the Central Connector from the regional transportation plan after Edgewood invoked an existing law that allowed any city in Orange County to stop a highway going through it.

In 1999, Edgewood adopted a beautification program, beginning with decorative signs at the city limits. Future plans included traffic calming roundabouts on some city streets, decorative street lights, buried utility lines, and storm water and sewer improvements. Edgewood banned truck traffic except deliveries on some streets within the city limits, but because the main street doubles as a state highway, street beautification presents a challenge. For about two miles in Edgewood the highway splits into Orange Avenue southbound and Hansel Avenue northbound.

Edgewood annexed several contiguous Orange County neighborhoods in the 1990s, doubling the city's size. Its population of 1,901 in 2000 was 90 percent white, 5 percent black, and 8 percent Hispanic. Edgewood remains primarily a residential community, with retail, commercial, and some industrial land use along Orange Avenue.

GOLDENROD

BY GARRET KREMER-WRIGHT

The exact boundaries of Goldenrod have perplexed people over the years mainly because this unincorporated community is surrounded by four towns: Casselberry, Oviedo, Orlando, and Winter Park. To further confuse matters, Goldenrod straddles both Orange and Seminole counties. Even if the boundaries are questionable, the history is not.

As one can accurately surmise, Goldenrod received its name from the wildflower. The name was first used in the 1880s by Elmer J. Beidler when he planted the first citrus trees in the area. In the early beginnings, the town was seen as the countryside, and, even as the surrounding areas began to fill up with residents, Goldenrod was able to keep its country feel. The town really came into existence in March 1926, when five New York businessmen founded the Golden Rod Corporation and bought 158 lots that bordered the Winter Park-Oviedo Road (now Aloma/SR-426). Unfortunately for them, the Depression scared many prospective buyers away. However, President Franklin D. Roosevelt's New Deal programs kept Goldenrod alive. Between 1936 and 1939 the Rural Electrification Program brought electricity to the area, and the Works Progress Administration improved Dike, Floyd (now Bear Gully), and Dodd Roads.

In 1951, a post office was established with Walter Spelzhausen as the first postmaster. A few years later in 1958, the town had its own volunteer fire department. The department became a paid district in 1966 and a year later, the Goldenrod-Dommerich Fire Department was established with Bill Ward as its first fire chief. Road improvements began in the 1960s when Semoran Boulevard (SR 436) was completed. The major road improvement for Goldenrod was the expansion of Aloma Avenue from Semoran to Howell Branch Road from two to four lanes. This project began in 1977 and was completed two years later. Upon its completion, the town celebrated by throwing the first Goldenrod Festival in January 1979. The festival continues to this day. In 1980, Goldenrod boasted twenty-six subdivisions, thirty-three apartment complexes, three elementary schools, a middle school, and the University of Central Florida. It also had sixteen churches and numerous civic organizations (such as Goldenrod Civic Club).

In 2000, twenty-two blocks of downtown were designated a part of the Associate Main Street program. The Goldenrod Fire Station and Museum opened in October 2002. The building contains offices for the Goldenrod Historical Society, Chamber of Commerce and Goldenrod Historic Village, and the fire station museum.

GOTHA

BY TANA MOSIER PORTER

The Ed Bann, Frank Murray, and Gus Mohr families lived in the woods on Lake Olivia, about nine miles west of Orlando, before the woods became Gotha. Henry A. Hempel, a German from Buffalo, New York, visited the settlement in 1876. He returned and purchased 1,000 acres of land, built a log cabin, cleared the land, planted citrus trees, and sent for his family. Henry P. Belknap spent a few months in the area in 1878 and returned to live there in 1879. Hempel laid out a town plat, recorded in 1885, that encompassed the land he homesteaded, and land homesteaded by Henry Belknap, John and Eliza Mohr, and Eugene Friedrich. He named it Gotha, for his birthplace in Germany. Residents made no move to incorporate the town, depending on Orange County for government.

Henry Hempel opened a grocery store and paid to have Gotha's mail brought from the nearest post office in Orlando. With a hotel, one store, and numerous dwellings under construction, he

Palm Cottage Gardens was home to Henry Nehrling's experimental botanical garden. At the turn of the twentieth century, Palm Cottage Gardens doubled as a popular destination for thousands of tourists including Theodore Roosevelt and Thomas Edison.

PHOTO BY JOHN BRADLEY

ordered a saw, shingle, and planing mill from Pennsylvania, and set up a sawmill to provide employment. Hempel owned the first mule team in Gotha. He wrote a promotional pamphlet entitled, "On the Back Bone of Florida—Gotha, New Colony, Orange County, Florida," which he circulated in large northern cities. His pamphlet attracted a number of families who bought land and settled in Gotha, among them, B. Huppel, also a native of Gotha, Germany. The L. Hartman, Harry Moore, H. A. Regener, and L. Wichtendahl families followed, as did a group from Cincinnati, Ohio.

Henry Belknap, who had taught school in Orlando in 1882, began teaching in a log cabin in Gotha in 1883. The town built a schoolhouse in 1885. When Gotha's post office opened in 1883, Belknap became the first postmaster. The Germans established a Turnverein, an athletic institution with about thirty members, and built a hall in 1886 or 1887. A small group of German Lutherans began meeting in their homes about 1888, and the Reverend Carl Brommer came in 1891 to organize a church. The congregation of the Missouri Synod built the Zion Lutheran Church in 1894. The arrival of the Florida Midland Railroad in 1888 provided for the shipment north of Gotha citrus fruit and brought wealthy winter visitors from northern cities to Gotha.

Well-educated Germans enjoyed an active social life in Gotha, which Henry Hempel had originally intended to become a community of free thinkers. Poet Frank Siller, from Milwaukee, Wisconsin, purchased forty acres in 1883 for horticulturalist and writer Henry Nehrling. Nehrling arrived by train in 1886 to work on his land and, for the

Right: The front cover of Henry Hempel's pamphlet which encouraged northerners to move to Gotha.

COURTESY OF THE ORANGE COUNTY REGIONAL HISTORY CENTER.

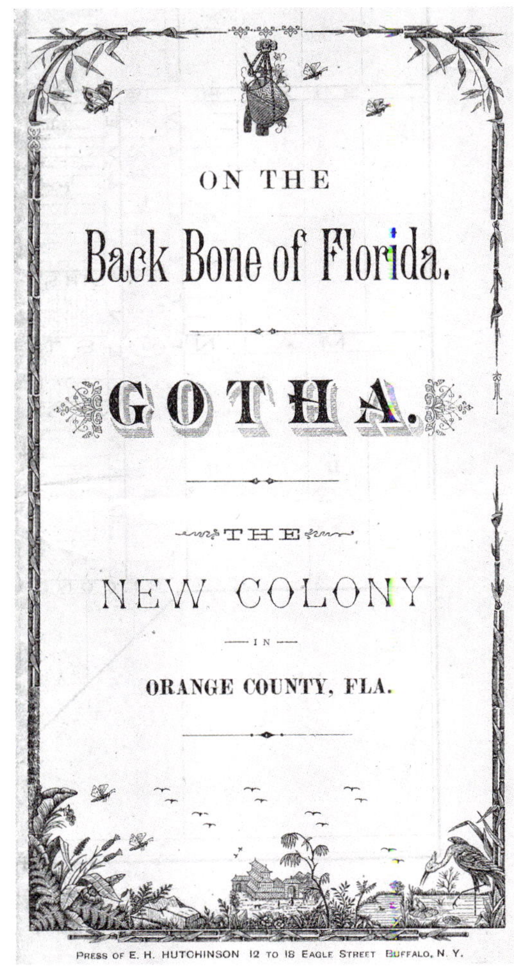

Below: Hempel's pamphlet also contained a full-page map of the town.

COURTESY OF THE ORANGE COUNTY REGIONAL HISTORY CENTER.

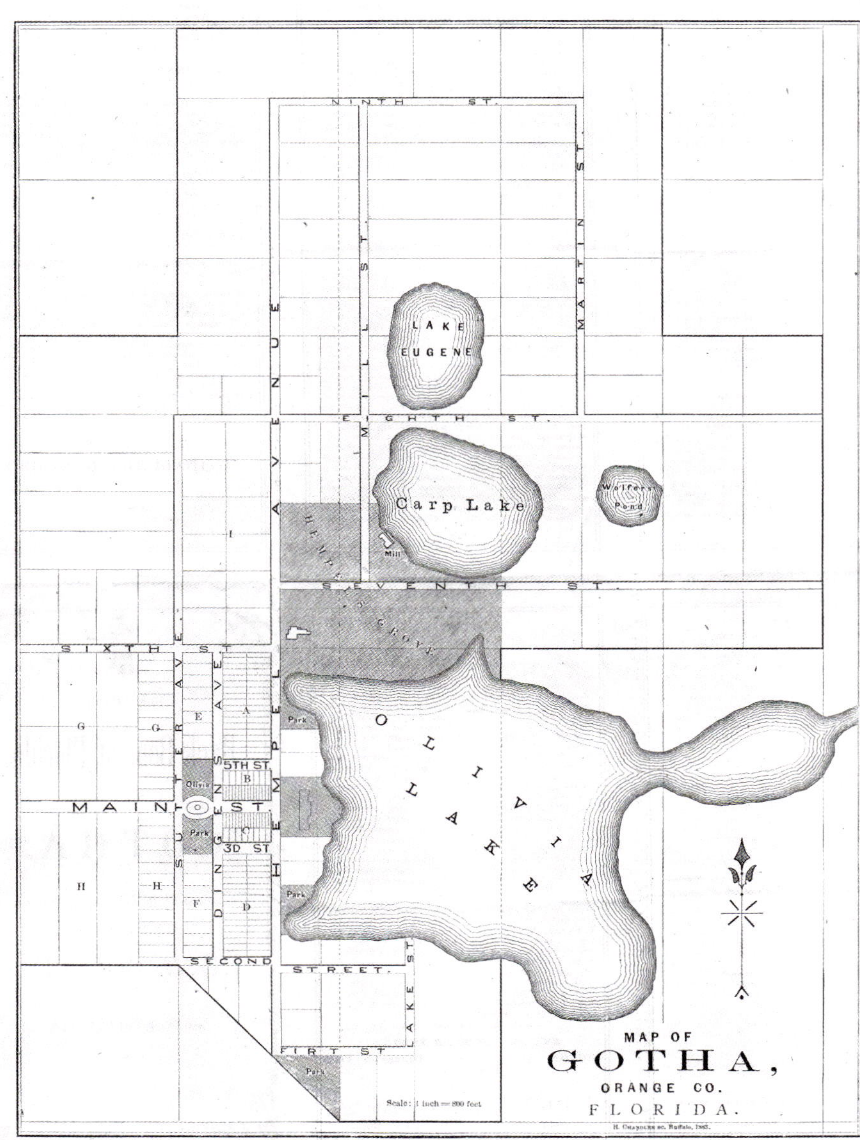

following decade, he spent one or two months each winter in Gotha. He cleared land for oranges and built a small house in the late 1880s, calling it "Palm Cottage Gardens." Nehrling moved his family from Milwaukee in 1902. A world-recognized scientist by 1887, Henry Nehrling gained fame for the caladiums and bromeliads he developed in Gotha.

Residents considered but did not pursue incorporation in the 1920s. The town remained small and rural, even as citrus groves gave way to housing developments. The population in 1990 stood at 265. When Orange County amended its charter to allow such communities to protect themselves with a rural settlement designation preventing annexations without the approval of the county board and the majority of the registered voters in the district, Gotha moved in 1995 to establish the "Gotha Rural Settlement" as a preservation district.

In 2000, the population had grown to 731, with 83 percent white, 7 percent Hispanic, and 4 percent black. During World War II, German prisoners of war held at camps in Central Florida attended church in Gotha, where the German influence remained strong and hymns might be sung in German. In the 2000 census, 27 percent of Gotha's residents still claimed German ancestry.

This birth record of the Koehne children illustrates the strong German heritage of Gotha's residents.

COURTESY OF THE ORANGE COUNTY REGIONAL HISTORY CENTER

Gotha, Orange Co., Florida, ...189

Wochentage der Geburtstage in der Familie von Herrn Chs. Koehne in Gotha, Florida

Chs. Koehne	geboren	July 28	1833.	Sonntag
Minna	"	"	Oct 19	1840.	Montag

Kinder

George Koehne		"	Oct 8	1858	Freitag
Armin	"	"	Aug 19	1860	Sonntag
Louis	"	"	Dec 12	1863	Samstag
Willy	"	"	Apr 2	1867	Dienstag
Anna	"	"	Dec 18	1869	Samstag
Minna	"	"	Juni 9	1873	Montag
Lillie	"	"	Aug 16	1874	Sonntag
Adele	"	"	" 9	1876	Mitwoch
Alma	"	"	Sep 30	1879	Dienstag

Lake Buena Vista

BY STEPHANIE GAUB

Walt Disney held a press conference in November 1965 to announce his plans to build a new theme park near Orlando.

COURTESY OF THE ORANGE COUNTY REGIONAL HISTORY CENTER.

Lake Buena Vista is most recognizable as the home of the Walt Disney World Resort; however, it is also home to fifteen residents—Disney employees and their immediate families. Located approximately one mile north of Downtown Disney, it is one of two Florida municipalities controlled by The Walt Disney World Company, the other being the city of Bay Lake. Its city status is confusing to many, and to truly understand the history of Lake Buena Vista, one must first know the history of Walt Disney World and the Reedy Creek Improvement District.

In 1959, Walt Disney began looking for a location to build a second theme park. Marketing had shown that only 2 percent of Disneyland's visitors came from east of the Mississippi River, where 75 percent of the population lived. In addition to Orlando, Disney looked at sites near St. Louis, Niagara Falls, Baltimore/Washington, D.C. area, and Ocala, Florida, as the home of his new theme park. He chose land just south of Orlando because of the attraction area's year-round sunshine and warmth as well as its easy access via Florida's Turnpike and Interstate 4. Once the site was chosen, the plans were set in motion to develop the thirty thousand acres that the Walt Disney Company purchased from area landowners.

In 1967, Governor Claude Kirk signed laws that allowed the Walt Disney Company to incorporate the City of Reedy Creek, create the Reedy Creek Improvement District, and incorporate the city of Bay Lake. Two years later, the governor approved a law which redefined the boundaries of the City of Reedy Creek, and the town's name was changed to Lake Buena Vista. The latter name was chosen as Reedy Creek no longer flowed through the city.

Today the Improvement District is made up of 25,000 acres (18,800 are located in Orange County while 6,000 are located in Osceola County) and is the site of the Walt Disney World Resort Complex, Lake Buena Vista, and Bay Lake. According to the District's website, Reedy Creek is "...a special taxing district...[that] must operate in accordance with its charter and state laws governing such districts. Just as any city or county, the income is derived from taxes and fees imposed within its boundaries. In the case of the Reedy Creek Improvement District, the major portion of taxes are paid to the District by Walt Disney World Company and other property owners, who also pay property taxes to Orange and Osceola Counties." The District is governed by a five-person board of supervisors, a district administrator, and a deputy district administrator.

Though Lake Buena Vista is unique in its structure and governance, its importance to the vitality of Orange County cannot be understated. Its proximity to the Walt Disney World Complex makes it an ideal location for hotels, restaurants, and other businesses related to the tourism industry. The tiny town of fifteen plays host to thousands of guests every year, securing its economic impact on the history of Orange County.

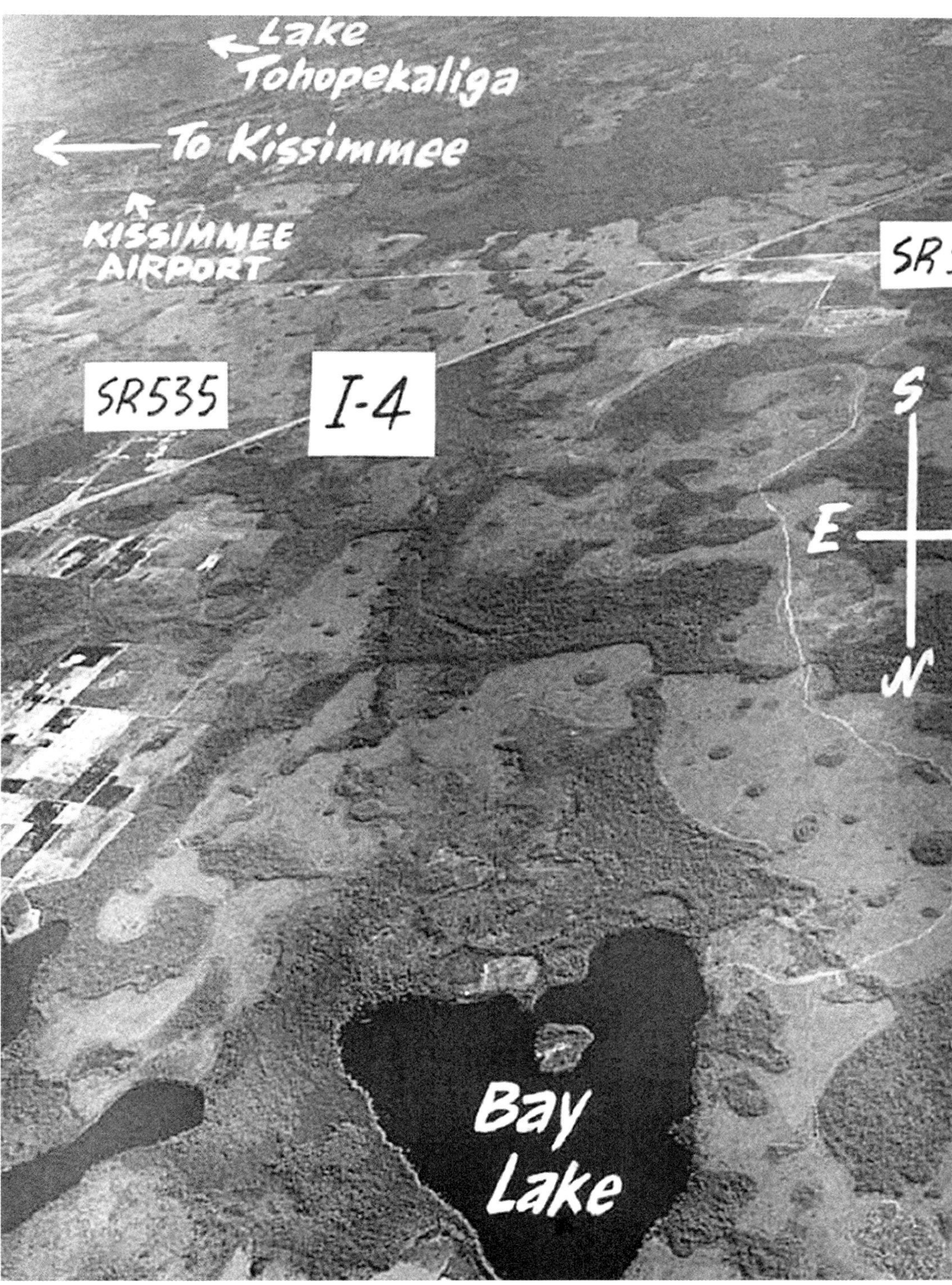

This picture of the land that now comprises Walt Disney World was taken on December 6, 1965.

COURTESY OF THE ORANGE COUNTY REGIONAL HISTORY CENTER

MAITLAND

BY BARBARA KNOWLES

Jules André Smith founded the Research Studio in 1938 as an art colony. Now known as the Maitland Art Center, his vision continues through the Center's exhibitions, resident artists, art instruction, and community programming. The complex is one of the South's few surviving examples of "fantasy" architecture. Its twenty-three separate structures feature Mayan/Aztec motifs.

PHOTO BY JOHN BRADLEY

The earliest Orange County towns formed around forts, which explains why Maitland was a small community well before the railroad came in 1880. Fort Maitland was one of a chain of military stockades built in Central Florida during the Second Seminole War (1835-1842). In 1838 the fort, named in honor of Captain William Seton Maitland, was constructed on the west side of what is now Lake Maitland.

Born in New York City in 1798, Maitland descended from a long line of Scottish nobility and, after attending the U.S. Military Academy at West Point, he was commissioned as a second lieutenant. He fought in the Second Seminole War's first and deadliest battle, commonly referred to as Dade's Massacre, on the Withlacooche River December 31, 1835. Despite the name, he survived, but later, severely wounded from another battle and despondent because he had to leave his men, he jumped from a ship in Savannah Harbor and drowned.

On August 4, 1842, the government passed into law the Florida Armed Occupation Act in which grants were provided for up to 160 acres of land to each head of household who was willing to clear and cultivate five acres the first year and build a house within the same time. In addition, he or his heirs were required to live on the property for a minimum of five years. With the Second Seminole War coming to an end (officially August 14, 1842) and tired of trying to remove Seminole Indians from the territory, the government hoped that the Act would encourage new homesteaders to fight the remaining Indians.

When settlers arrived in 1843, they found the fort in ruins, but by 1872, the community had enough residents to warrant a post office. One of the most important people in those early years to

homestead the area was Isaac Vanderpool, who, with the help of George H. and Dr. Richard Packwood, laid out the town of Maitland.

Vanderpool was a New Yorker who traveled extensively throughout South America before coming to Maitland. On his trip home from Brazil in 1870, his sailboat anchored in Jacksonville for provisions, allowing him and his companion, H. S. Kedney, to travel up the St. Johns River to Fort Maitland. Vanderpool secured a 160-acre property and hired Kedney to homestead the land and turn it into an orange grove. Vanderpool left for New York but returned with his bride, Harriet Langman, in 1876 to live on Lake Maitland. He operated the town's first packing house and, with Kedney's additional assistance, planted numerous oaks in order to beautify the community.

Also key to the early development of Maitland was William H. Waterhouse, a master carpenter, who moved to Maitland for health reasons. While spending thirteen months in the infamous Andersonville prison in Georgia during the Civil War, he suffered from neglect and malnutrition. In 1884, he moved his family into a stately house he built on Lake Lily. Waterhouse built many homes and churches in Maitland and served his community as an alderman when Maitland became incorporated in 1885. He retained the position for thirty-six years.

Born in Timmonsville, South Carolina, but raised in Maitland, Carl Hill Galloway led his town and the surrounding communities of Winter Park and Altamonte Springs, among others, into the twentieth century by establishing the Maitland Winter Park Telephone Exchange in 1910. The operation began as a smart business move to improve customer service for his father's grocery store. He installed telephones in the homes of the grocery's customers so that they could phone in orders. By 1915, the service had achieved such demand that he began charging. Six years later, the entrepreneur incorporated the telephone company and moved into a small building in Winter Park where he renamed the service the Winter Park Telephone Company, the title the company maintained until it joined United Telephone of Florida in 1979.

The James Erwin Hill family moved to Maitland in 1872 after filing for a 160-acre homestead. The Hill's second son, Sumpter Brock, became instrumental to the Florida citrus industry when he introduced new varieties of citrus to the state. After graduating from the University of Florida and Vanderbilt University, Sumpter toured Europe and discovered an array of different kinds of citrus in Italy. He returned to Maitland, imported foreign varieties of citrus, and opened two nurseries that specialized in establishing young trees.

Above: The crest of the Maitland family after which the town was named.

COURTESY OF THE ORANGE COUNTY REGIONAL HISTORY CENTER

Below: William H. Waterhouse built this home in 1884. It is listed on the National Register of Historic Places and is operated as a historic house museum by the Maitland Historical Society.

PHOTO BY JOHN BRADLEY

Above: Lake Lily Drive was the first direct route from Northeastern Florida to Maitland. When it was paved with brick in 1913, it became the first grouted brick road in Florida. In 1927 it became part of the Dixie Highway when it was joined with Black Bear Trail.

PHOTO BY JOHN BRADLEY

Below: The plight of the snowy egret worried Clara Dommerich, leading to the formation of the state Audubon Society in Maitland.

COURTESY OF THE NATIONAL AUDUBON SOCIETY

Another Maitland resident to put his stamp on Florida was Louis F. Dommerich, a wealthy silk merchant from New York who made the area his winter home. In 1891, he purchased 210 acres of land in Maitland and constructed a thirty-room mansion surrounded by 130 acres of landscaped grounds and 72 acres of citrus trees he named "Hiawatha Groves." The grounds included eight miles of boardwalk-like trails, a man-made pond, and its own citrus packing house. Today, this land constitutes the housing development Dommerich Estates.

However, the Dommerich's most far reaching contribution was the creation of the Florida Audubon Society. George Bird Grinnell was responsible for founding what was to become the National Audubon Society when as editor of *Forest and Stream* in 1886, he appealed to his readers to unite for bird preservation and protection. Within a year, thirty-nine thousand individuals joined the organization he named after the famous naturalist and painter John James Audubon. The list of early officers included: New York Governor and later U.S. President Theodore Roosevelt, Florida Governor W. D. Bloxham, American Museum of Natural History's Frank Chapman, Rollins College President G. M. Ward, Stetson University President J. F. Forbes, and the editors of the state's largest newspapers. A little later, the list grew to include President Grover Cleveland, Florida Governor W. S. Jennings, ornithologist Theodore S. Palmer, and Maria R. Audubon.

Louis and Clara Dommerich's interest in conservation may have begun when the couple learned that during the winter of 1900, 130,000 birds were shipped from the state to northern manufacturers, where their feathers were used primarily for women's hats.

In Maitland, the first meeting of the Florida chapter met at the Dommerich estate on March 2, 1900. That same year, working together, the state Audubon Societies successfully pushed for the passage of the Lacey Act, prohibiting the interstate trade of wildlife killed in violation of state laws.

The state headquarters is still in Maitland and the Audubon Center for Birds of Prey opened there as well in 1979. On June 14, 1979, Doris Mager, an Audubon staffer, perched herself in an inactive bald eagle nest on which she stayed for six days and five nights to raise awareness of the plight of the bald eagle and to raise money for the establishment of the Center. Dedicated volunteers treat nearly 700 birds of prey each year.

Ocoee

BY GARRET KREMER-WRIGHT

Originally called Starke Lake, Ocoee took its name from Dr. J. D. Starke, one of the area's earliest settlers. When the town was platted in 1886, Captain B. M. Sims changed the name of the town to Ocoee. The name came from a river near where he grew up in Tennessee. During the 1880s the Sea Board Air Line and Florida Midland Railroad (later Atlantic Coast Line) laid track through town. In 1880, the first school opened with Mrs. E. D. Perkins as the teacher. By 1880 the town had become the center of social, economic, and political activities

The town gained national attention on November 2, 1920, when the ten-hour Ocoee Race Riot occurred. This single event caused decades of turmoil. The circumstances surrounding the riot are still debated by historians. During this time, Ocoee was divided into three quarters, Northern,

The Withers-Maguire House was built in 1888 by Confederate Veteran William Temple Withers. In 1910, Martha Withers sold the house to David Maguire. The Maguire family lived in the home until 1983.

PHOTO BY JOHN BRADLEY

Above: The Marshall Farm in Ocoee produced cucumbers.

COURTESY OF THE ORANGE COUNTY REGIONAL HISTORY CENTER

Below: The Ocoee Christian Church was built in 1891 by General William T. Withers and is the oldest church building in continual use in Central Florida. The church's stained glass windows were shipped from Belgium to Sanford, Florida. From there they were shipped to Ocoee by ox cart.

PHOTO BY JOHN BRADLEY

Southern, and Central. African Americans lived in all of the sections but were primarily located in the Northern and Southern sections. Several months prior to the riot, two prominent Republican officials, Judge John M. Cheney and W. R. O'Neal held secret meetings in the Northern section of town to encourage African Americans to vote in the upcoming election. This move was strongly opposed by the Democratic Party, Ku Klux Klan, and the White Voters Executive Committee. Each of these groups tried to dissuade blacks from casting their vote. At each election a poll tax had to be paid in order to vote. A scheme was devised by these groups that on election day Justice of the Peace Robert Bigalow would vote early and then go fishing in Orlando. This ensured that any black who went to vote and was denied would have to travel to Orlando.

One such African American, Moses Norman, tried to vote without paying his poll tax and was denied. After being turned away he drove to Orlando and met with Judge Cheney to discuss his options. He was soon back in Ocoee demanding that he be allowed to vote. Norman was again denied. After his second denial, he went home and grabbed his shotgun. As he passed Hoyle Pounds' garage, an unidentified white man saw the gun and questioned him. The man called Constable Bernie Cannon and, when he saw that the gun was loaded, he pistol-whipped Norman and sent him home. The African American account argues that it was another prominent black, July Perry, who was denied the right to vote. History may never know whether it was Perry or Norman who tried to vote.

After the polls closed word reached a small gathering of white men at the local grocery store that several blacks were congregating at the home of July Perry. Wanting to put a stop to a potential riot, Sam T. Salisbury led a posse to arrest the two for attempting to vote. Some of the posse went to Norman's house to arrest him, while the majority went to Perry's. When Salisbury arrived at Perry's home to try and arrest him a melee ensued and shots were fired. When the dust settled two white men, Elmer McDaniel and Leo Borgard, lay dead while six others were wounded, including Salisbury. Perry was also wounded when he was struck on the head by Salisbury's Enfield rifle. He attempted to flee but was arrested and taken to jail. The rest of the blacks that were in Perry's house escaped through a trap door and into an adjacent cane field.

Word spread to the towns of Winter Garden and Orlando about the shooting and hundreds of white men jumped into their cars and headed to Ocoee to help. The mob quickly swelled to over 500 men, who retaliated for the shooting of McDaniel and Borgard by burning 25 African American homes, two churches, and a Masonic Lodge. Eight African Americans were also killed, including July Perry who was lynched by a mob of over one hundred men. The riot drove all the African Americans out of Ocoee with just the clothes on their backs. Order was finally restored on November 3. A substantial African American population would not return to Ocoee until the 1970s and 1980s.

Calm finally settled over Ocoee and people went back to doing their daily routine. Nearly three years later on November 23, 1923, the first meeting to incorporate Ocoee took place in Pounds Packing House. The city received its charter in May 1925. With the evolution of Ocoee into a city, the landscape began to change as well. Ocoee had primarily been an agricultural town in its early years but, its charter brought about a building and population boom. During World War II Ocoee sent more men per capita to the military than any other city in the United States. Also, areas around Starke Lake were used as campsites for the soldiers. It is interesting to note that the town was rarely mentioned in maps, telephone directories, and road signs. It was more common for people to hear about the neighboring cities of Winter Park and Apopka, even though both had smaller populations. Growth began in Ocoee during the 1970s and 1980s with the construction of businesses and a community center. By 1996, Ocoee had become the third fastest growing and third largest city in Orange County.

Ocoee again made headlines in 1980, when City Manager John Vignetti brought up the question of the legality of de-annexation from Orange County to become the sixty-eighth county in Florida. He argued that the town was not getting adequate services for the $325,000 in taxes being paid to the county. When the legality was looked into, it was found that only the Florida Legislature could create a new county. Thus the matter was dropped. While the 1920 race riot remains shrouded in mystery, Ocoee has moved on. The city has expanded its boundaries and built new facilities to help attract new residents to the community. Ocoee has a bright future ahead.

A land grant issued to Bluford M. Sims on October 5, 1883, for land in Ocoee.

COURTESY OF THE ORANGE COUNTY REGIONAL HISTORY CENTER.

(4—406.)

THE UNITED STATES OF AMERICA,

To all to whom these presents shall come, Greeting:

CERTIFICATE No. 3158 } Whereas Bluford M. Sims of Orange County Florida has deposited in the GENERAL LAND OFFICE of the United States a Certificate of the Register of the Land Office at Gainesville Florida whereby it appears that Full Payment has been made by the said Bluford M. Sims according to the provisions of the Act of Congress of the 24th of April, 1820, entitled "An Act making further provision for the sale of the Public Lands," and the acts supplemental thereto, for the north east quarter of the south east quarter of section twenty in township twenty two south of range twenty eight east of Tallahassee Meridian in Florida containing thirty nine acres and eighty one hundredths of an acre

according to the Official Plat of the Survey of the said lands, returned to the GENERAL LAND OFFICE by the Surveyor General, which said Tract has been purchased by the said Bluford M. Sims

Now know ye, That the United States of America, in consideration of the premises, and in conformity with the several Acts of Congress in such case made and provided, Have given and granted, and by these presents Do give and grant, unto the said Bluford M. Sims and to his heirs, the said Tract above described; To have and to hold the same, together with all the rights, privileges, immunities, and appurtenances, of whatsoever nature, thereunto belonging, unto the said Bluford M. Sims and to his heirs and assigns forever.

In testimony whereof, I, Chester A. Arthur, President of the United States of America, have caused these letters to be made Patent, and the seal of the General Land Office to be hereunto affixed.

Given under my hand, at the City of Washington, the fifth day of October, in the year of our Lord one thousand eight hundred and eighty three, and of the Independence of the United States the one hundred and eighth.

By the President: Chester A. Arthur

By M. H. Crook, Secretary.

S. W. Clark, Recorder of the General Land Office.

RECORDED, Vol. 5, Page 62

An aerial view of Downtown Orlando with Lake Eola in the foreground, c. 1930.

COURTESY OF THE ORANGE COUNTY REGIONAL HISTORY CENTER.

ORLANDO

BY TANA MOSIER PORTER

The City of Orlando came into existence in 1857, when it became the county seat of Orange County. The new town grew up along the western shore of Lake Eola, about four miles north of Fort Gatlin, one of the line of forts the Army established across the unsettled Central Florida wilderness during the Second Seminole War. Built in 1838, Fort Gatlin drew the first settlers to the Orlando area. In order to secure the territory when the war ended in 1842, the government offered land under the Armed Occupation Act to homesteaders who agreed to live near the forts and help protect the settlements if Indians attacked.

Brothers, Aaron and Isaac Jernigan, arrived from Georgia in the summer of 1842 to homestead property on Lake Holden near Fort Gatlin. They brought with them slaves and seven hundred head of cattle. Their wives and children joined them in 1843. Vincent Lee moved to the area late in 1842, and the Lowery and Marston families and several others followed by 1849. In 1850 a post office opened in Aaron Jernigan's house in the small settlement then known as Jernigan.

Aaron Jernigan's daughter, Martha Jernigan Tyler, later wrote of her experiences growing up on the Florida frontier. Woods covered the area when she arrived in 1843, and, other than the Indians, her nearest neighbors lived miles away on Lake Monroe. Mrs. Tyler recalled the abundance of game, and varmints: wolves, bears, wildcats, and panthers, also known as tigers. She described an Indian uprising in 1849 that resulted in the settlers being "forted up" for a year in Jernigan's stockade. Martha Tyler's memories of Christmas included feasting on wild turkey, deer, and bear meat, with wine made from the oranges growing wild around Lake Holden. The adults, men and women, enjoyed tobacco and snuff, and the children had candy sticks. The day concluded with music and dancing.

During the 1850s, James J. Patrick settled near Lake Conway and William A. Lovell started a steam sawmill on Lake Eola. John R. Worthington built the first log house near Lake Eola and also sold merchandise. James G. Speer settled on a farm near Lake Ivanhoe in 1854. William B. Hull, James P. Hughey, and Andrew Barber came with their families and slaves in 1855.

The handful of residents lived scattered among the pine forests and lakes in 1856, when the county electorate voted to move the seat of government to the settlement at Fort Gatlin. The state legislature had established the county seat at Mellonville in 1845, but in 1856, Orange County voters decided to relocate it. Fort Gatlin tallied the most votes because Judge James G. Speer manipulated the outcome of the election. Aware that soldiers could vote wherever they happened to be on election day, he invited a company of soldiers stationed in Sumter County to a picnic at Fort Gatlin and persuaded them to vote while they were in town.

County leaders looking for a location for a courthouse soon discovered that not many people lived near Fort Gatlin and that the sparse and scattered population actually lived closer to Lake Eola. They concluded that Fort Gatlin no longer served as the community nucleus and questioned whether it should be the county seat. Land speculator B.F. Caldwell settled the developing controversy with a gift of four acres of land for a new court house near Lake Eola in what is now downtown Orlando. The Jernigan Post Office closed, and in 1857 a new post office called Orlando opened near the new court house site.

The question of why and how the name of the hero in Shakespeare's *As You Like It* got to the settlement on the Florida frontier in 1857 has no known answer. The traditional story, and the most colorful, has a soldier named Orlando Reeves dying while standing sentry near Lake Eola in 1835, during the Second Seminole War. According to the legend, he was able to warn the sleeping soldiers of a

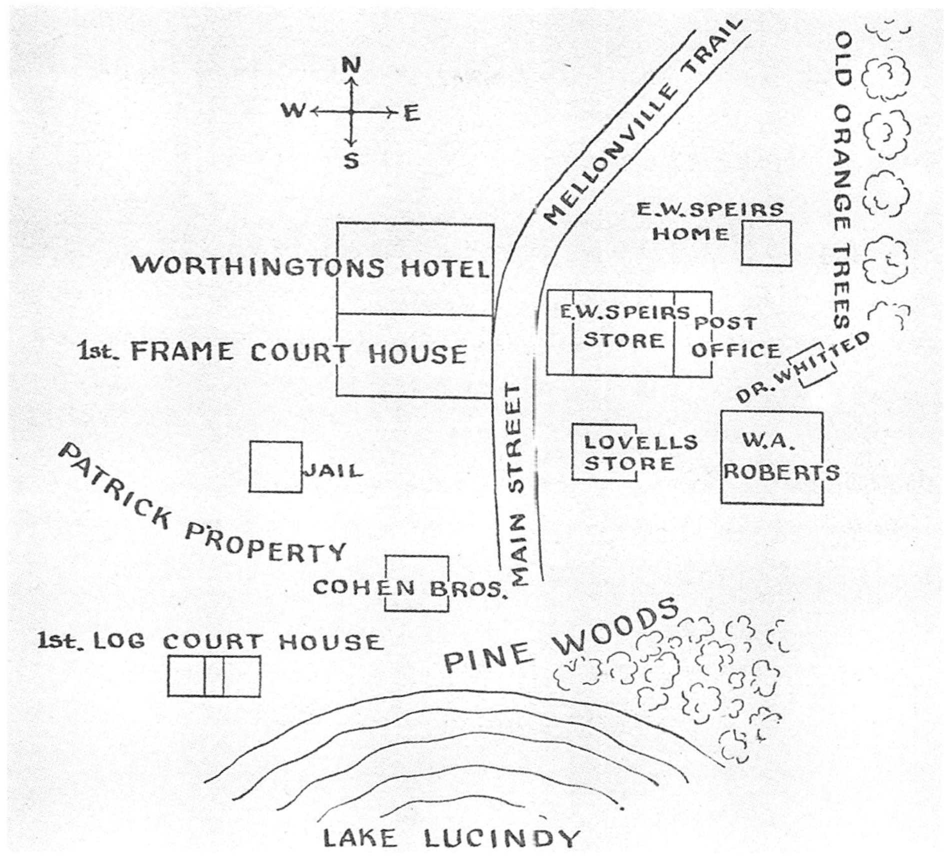

Above: Kena Fries drew this map of Orlando and included it in her book Orlando In The Long, Long Ago, And Now. *It depicts the town as it appeared in 1857.*

COURTESY OF THE ORANGE COUNTY REGIONAL HISTORY CENTER.

Left: Martha Jernigan Tyler, daughter of Orlando pioneer Aaron Jernigan, unveiled the Daughters of the American Revolution marker commemorating the site of Fort Gatlin on March 27, 1924. Mrs. Tyler died two years later.

COURTESY OF THE ORANGE COUNTY REGIONAL HISTORY CENTER

Above: On January 13, 1939, students from Cherokee Jr. High School presented this marker to the City of Orlando. The marker honors Orlando Reeves, for whom many believe the city was named.
COURTESY OF THE ORANGE COUNTY REGIONAL HISTORY CENTER.

Below: The oldest existing photograph of Orlando shows the intersection of Orange Avenue and Central Boulevard, c. 1875.
COURTESY OF THE ORANGE COUNTY REGIONAL HISTORY CENTER.

coming attack before falling himself. The existence of such a soldier or even a skirmish is doubtful, but more than a century later, in 1939, students at Cherokee Junior High School collected money to place a marker at the site where the grave was thought to be, commemorating the man in whose honor they believed Orlando was named.

Another theory credits pioneer settler Judge Speer, who saw Central Florida as a veritable Forest of Arden. When the time came to name the new county seat, the influential Judge Speer suggested Orlando, the name of the romantic hero in Shakespeare's play, *As You Like It*, set in the Forest of Arden. In still another story, a planter from South Carolina, Orlando Savage Rees, owned land in Central Florida in the mid-nineteenth century. His descendants believe that Orlando was named for Orlando Rees. And according to yet another tale, a passing ox driver named Orlando died in the street from appendicitis, was buried where he fell, and thus gave the town its name. No one will ever know for sure why they named the place Orlando.

The county had no money to build a courthouse, so until 1863 they held court in an old deserted two-room log cabin in the pine woods just east of the old Church Street depot. It had a dirt floor and no windows. One room became the county offices, and the other served as Orlando's first schoolroom. Religious groups, Baptists, Methodists, Episcopalians, and later, Presbyterians, shared the schoolroom on Sundays.

Orange County replaced the original log courthouse with a two-story frame building in 1863. Three more courthouses eventually occupied the site provided by Benjamin Caldwell, and for nearly 140 years the seat of Orange County government remained at the corner of Central Avenue and Main Street (now Magnolia Avenue).

Orlando had little interest in the Civil War. Most of the city's fourteen slaves continued to work, sharing the hardships and shortages of the war. The Orlando Post Office closed when Florida joined the Confederacy, reopening in 1866 after Florida returned to the Union. During the war Mrs. Hull served as unofficial postmistress, distributing mail from the boarding house she ran while her husband fought with the Confederate Army.

New communities on the American frontiers, West or South, measured progress in institutions, such as schools, churches, Masonic Lodges, and infrastructure, including paving and street lighting, and water and sewer provisions. These evidences of Orlando's growth began to appear by the late 1860s. In 1866 the settlement comprised four houses, four stores, a barroom, and the court house. One of the houses operated as Lovell's Hotel. In 1868 the Orange County Board of Education met to plan future schools. E.W. Speir became postmaster in 1871, and in his one-story frame store building, at Pine and Main Streets, the post office found its first permanent location. It remained there until 1889.

The Union Church, planned since 1857, finally was built in 1872. During the week it served as a school and, on Sundays, various denominations held religious services in the building. A Masonic Lodge first met in Orlando in 1876.

Orlando incorporated as a city in 1875. The twenty-two voters in a total population of eighty-five placed the boundaries in a square, creating a four-acre Original Town, with the Orange County Courthouse at its center, one mile from each of its boundary streets. William J. Brack became the first mayor. The Town Council met for the first time on August 4, 1875, with the mayor and seven aldermen. In July 1879, the town council settled a city charter legality question by dissolving the corporation established by the charter, and the City of Orlando ceased to exist. Three months later the council met again as usual. Who governed in the interim and how and why the city reorganized remain unknown.

A newspaper started in 1875. Trees still grew in some streets the following year, when the new town addressed issues of sanitation, ordering that the streets be cleaned and appointing a committee to select a site for a public well and privy. Individuals were encouraged to build sidewalks. In 1879 Thomas Shine built a large house at the corner of Orange Avenue and Jefferson Street, the first in Orlando with a bathroom.

Orlando's greatest growth occurred during several economic booms, the first following

Above: In 1891, the 1875 Orange County Courthouse was moved to make room for the new brick courthouse. In its new location, the wooden structure became part of the Tremont Hotel.

COURTESY OF THE ORANGE COUNTY REGIONAL HISTORY CENTER

Below: Passengers wait outside of the South Florida Railroad station in Orlando in 1886. This was the second station built for the railroad within Orlando.

COURTESY OF THE ORANGE COUNTY REGIONAL HISTORY CENTER

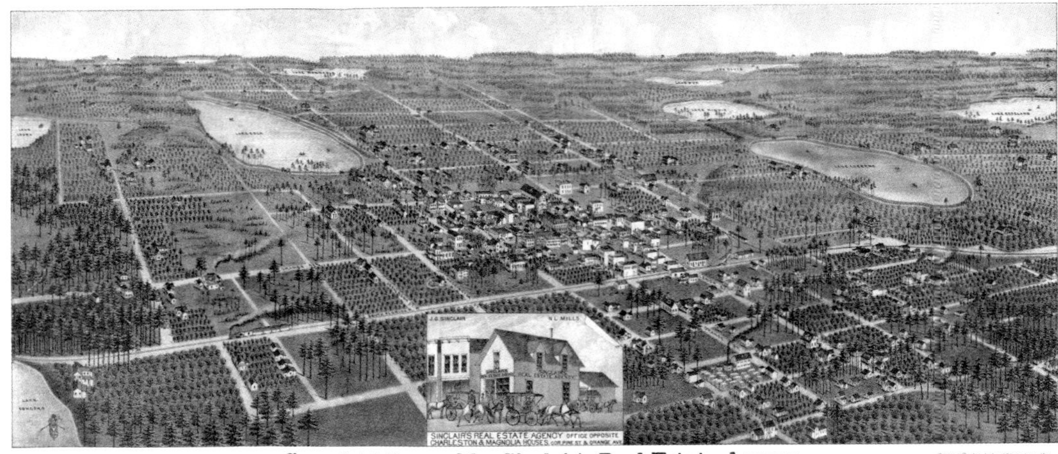

Above: An 1884 Orlando map.
COURTESY OF THE ORANGE COUNTY REGIONAL HISTORY CENTER.

Below: The sign on the front of this building reads "Elijah Hand Funeral Director/Furniture.
COURTESY OF THE ORANGE COUNTY REGIONAL HISTORY CENTER.

the arrival in 1880 of the South Florida Railroad. Until then, transportation remained one of the town's most serious deficiencies. In 1875 several citizens chartered the Lake Monroe and Orlando Railroad in an attempt to remedy the problem, but it made no progress until 1879, when it reorganized as the South Florida Railroad, with a new charter and new funding. The tracks reached Orlando on October 1, 1880, and on the following day the first train from Sanford arrived carrying railroad officials and prominent citizens. Regular service began in November 1880.

The railroad provided Orlando with much-needed transportation into and out of the town, but its location caused the business center to shift from the courthouse square at Central Avenue and Main Street, south and west toward the railroad, which ran along the western side of the settlement, between South Street and Colonial Drive. In 1881 a train station occupied the corner of West Church and Gertrude Streets. H. A. Luckie followed with the Lucky House hotel at the corner of Orange Avenue and Pine Street.

Mahlon Gore, who became the editor and publisher of the *Orange County Reporter*, walked through deep sand from Sanford to Orlando in 1880. He found a community of more than 200 people. The business district, consisting of four stores, one hotel, one blacksmith and wagon shop, and a livery stable, faced three sides of the courthouse square. The livery horse grazed in the surrounding woods. The best vehicle to be had was a buckboard, and that required two days' notice because the livery man had to go into the woods and hunt for the horse.

Gore also noted new saw mills, planing mills, and a beginning building boom in 1880. In 1883, the city ordered the construction of sidewalks, contracted for the removal of stumps from the streets, and began to collect garbage. Jacob Summerlin gave land that year for a park around Lake Eola, and a volunteer fire department started after a near fatal fire.

By 1884, Orlando boasted forty stores and three livery stables. With more than three hundred pupils, the school moved to the first floor of the Masonic Lodge building on Church Street two blocks from the railroad. Despite the progress, the streets remained unpaved with just a few board sidewalks. Cows grazed at large among mostly one-story buildings.

A fire in January 1884 destroyed most of the block between Pine and Central and Court and Main Streets, destroying several businesses, along with the offices and printing shop of the *Orange County Reporter*. After the fire, the city ordered that all buildings be brick. The Volunteer Fire Department reorganized in 1885 and acquired a truck pulled by borrowed horses.

A high wooden fence surrounded the new Orange County jail, built on the corner of Orange Avenue and Washington Street in 1884. Windows on one side of the San Juan Hotel, built in 1885, overlooked the jail yard and proved popular on the day of a hanging. The San Juan, Orlando's first permanent hotel, was the largest building in town when completed, and with additions and improvements over the years, it remained in business under the same name for nearly a century. Elijah Hand opened an undertaking business in 1885. Before his arrival, people who died in the morning were buried that afternoon, and people who died at night were buried the first thing the next morning.

Above: San Juan Hotel, 1884.

COURTESY OF THE ORANGE COUNTY REGIONAL HISTORY CENTER.

Below: The Myrtle Shop was a business located in the Parramore community during the 1950s.

COURTESY OF THE ORANGE COUNTY REGIONAL HISTORY CENTER.

Right: During the 1980s, Church Street Station was a popular tourist spot in downtown Orlando, boasting 1.7 million visitors in 1985. After years of despair, the site is once again home to restaurants and shops.
COURTESY OF THE ORANGE COUNTY REGIONAL HISTORY CENTER

Below: Orlando has been touting itself as a tourist destination since the early 1900s. This postcard was mailed in 1912.
COURTESY OF THE ORANGE COUNTY REGIONAL HISTORY CENTER

Around 1880, Sam Jones and his family established a home on the southeast side of the town, near a large sinkhole north of what became the Greenwood Cemetery. Other African American families followed, including several former slaves. Named Jonestown for its first residents, the community flourished as a black enclave until segregation and floods forced the residents to move across Orlando in 1941. On the west side of the city James Parramore platted a neighborhood in 1880 and built cottages to house the blacks employed in the households of white Orlandoans. The area grew to become Orlando's African American Parramore neighborhood.

Orlando's population increased from 200 in 1880 to 2,856 in 1890. Residents called it "The Phenomenal City" in 1886 but it still lacked the appearance of an urban community. Residences tended to be scattered, and many people lived outside the corporate limits, though some of the most impressive houses were in or near the business district. The Orlando Street Railway started in 1886 and the Orlando Water Works obtained a city franchise to provide water and forty-five fire hydrants. Telephones connected Orlando and Sanford that year. Between 1885 and 1895, the city planted oak trees to replace the virgin pine forest that had been cut several years earlier so that a grid system of streets could be platted.

Orlando's early economy centered on the cattle industry, but the railroad, renamed the Atlantic Coast Line in 1902, enabled citrus growers to ship fresh fruit to northern

markets, making Orlando a major citrus shipping center by 1890. Freezing weather in the winter of 1894-1895 ended Orlando's first boom. A hard freeze in December 1894 destroyed the fruit on the trees, and a second freeze in February 1895 killed the trees. Banks failed. More than half of the English Colony, who had immigrated to the area in the 1880s to grow citrus, gave up their groves south of Orlando and returned to England. It took fifteen years for the citrus industry to recover and during those years Orlando actually lost population, from 2,856 in 1890 to 2,481 in 1900.

"The Phenomenal City" became "The City Beautiful" in 1908. The population grew to 3,894 in 1910, as prosperity returned. Voters decided in 1913 to give up the municipal form of government in favor of the commission form, which combines legislative and executive functions. Commissioners replaced aldermen on January 1, 1914, and the mayor and commission system governs Orlando today.

By the 1920s, the automobile had pushed tourism to unprecedented heights and launched a new boom in Orlando that paralleled a national period of prosperity and progress. The automobile and improved highways brought increased tourism, the growth of business and construction, and the beginnings of suburbanization. Orlando issued a record number of building permits in 1925, with a total value of more than $9 million. New hotels and office buildings transformed the downtown, and Orlando had one hundred miles of brick paved streets by the end of the decade.

Caught up in the Great Florida Land Boom, investors bought real estate and sold it again almost overnight for quick and easy profits. The city expanded geographically, opening new streets and annexing subdivisions: Orwin Manor, Edgewater Heights, and Lorna Doone Park in 1924; Glendonjo Park, and Spring Lake Terrace in 1925; and Orlando Highlands, Country Club Estates, Princeton Court, Oakhurst Subdivision, Ivanhoe Plaza, several College Park additions, and Silver Lake Park, all in 1926. The boom collapsed in 1926, leaving some platted subdivisions with streets but no houses.

Twelve packing houses made Orlando the largest individual citrus fruit shipping center in Florida in 1926, as local companies marketed three-fourths of the state crop.

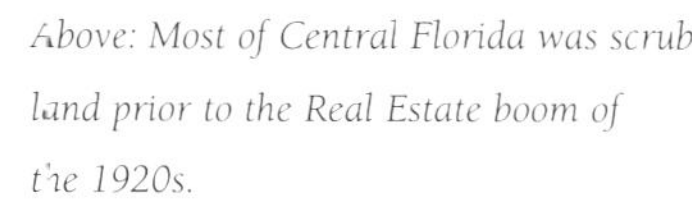

Above: Most of Central Florida was scrub land prior to the Real Estate boom of the 1920s.

COURTESY OF THE ORANGE COUNTY REGIONAL HISTORY CENTER.

Below: Several upscale pseudo-Spanish style homes were created as a part of the Spring Lake Terrace subdivision, now known simply as Spring Lake. Today, homes in this neighborhood sell for as much as $1.2 million.

COURTESY OF THE ORANGE COUNTY REGIONAL HISTORY CENTER.

Above: Orange Avenue, c. 1935.

COURTESY OF THE ORANGE COUNTY REGIONAL HISTORY CENTER.

Below: Orlando International Airport welcomes millions of visitors to Orlando.

COURTESY OF THE ORANGE COUNTY REGIONAL HISTORY CENTER.

Orlando's population, just over 9,000 in 1920, grew to more than 27,000 in 1930. By 1932 Orlando had 135 miles of brick paved streets and 38 hotels.

Parramore, the segregated black enclave on Orlando's west side, had by the 1930s developed into a strong and cohesive community with segregated schools, churches, and professional offices. Separate, but by no means equal, the neighborhood boasted owner-occupied homes and black-owned shops in a parallel African-American world. The Civil Rights Movement reached Orlando in 1960, with sit-ins at downtown lunch counters and stand-ins at local theaters. The city integrated slowly, but peacefully, due in part to the efforts of the Mayor's Advisory Committee on Interracial Relations or the Bi-Racial Committee. The schools desegregated last. Integration robbed Parramore businesses of their captive clientele, and school desegregation took children out of the neighborhood and closed community schools. The neighborhood declined into blight in the 1960s.

Aviation brought another economic boom, during and after World War II. Orlando's Municipal Airport, built in 1928, became the Orlando Army Air Base in 1940. The military built a second airfield near Pine Castle in 1941, which later became the McCoy Air Force Base and is now the Orlando International Airport. Thousands of airmen trained in Orlando for service overseas, and many returned to live here after the war. The aviation industry followed the military to Central Florida, and the U.S. Missile Test Center, established at Cape Canaveral in 1955, brought the aerospace industry. The

Martin Company, now Lockheed Martin, moved its headquarters to property south of Orlando, opening a plant there in 1958. The company brought scientists and engineers from Maryland and quickly became the area's leading employer.

Building marked the decade after the war, as Orlando progressed from provincial town to metropolitan center. Roads, hotels, hospitals, banks, and shopping centers changed forever the character of the small southern city. Venerable old downtown residences and commercial buildings disappeared to make space for parking lots near the stores. But the parking lots could not save downtown shopping after Colonial Plaza, the first shopping center, opened in 1956. Orlando's population, 36,736 in 1940, reached 51,826 by 1950, and 88,135 in 1960.

City leaders' economic development plans seemed successful by 1965, when light industry flourished in five industrial parks around Orlando's perimeter. The economic emphasis swung from light industry back to tourism with the opening of Interstate 4 through Orlando's downtown in 1965, and Walt Disney's announcement of his plans to build an entertainment complex south of Orlando.

Walt Disney selected Orlando for his new amusement park, Walt Disney World, which opened in 1971, because of its ideal weather and promising transportation. Other theme parks followed, creating an unprecedented economic boom. Tourism expanded dramatically, and hotels, restaurants, and gas stations multiplied. The downtown skyline began to look more urban with the rise of taller and taller buildings. Housing developments replaced orange groves, and Orlando's population, 99,006 in 1970, and 128,291 in 1980, grew to 164,674 in 1990 and to 185,951 in 2000. Growth changed Orlando's ethnic character as well. In 1950 the city was 71 percent native white and 25 percent African American. By 1970, the white population had fallen to 70 percent, while blacks had increased to 29.5 percent. In 1980, the numbers changed again, to 68 percent white, 30 percent black, 4 percent Hispanic. The 2000 Census revealed that 61 percent of Orlando's residents were white, 27 percent were African American, and 17.5 percent were Hispanic.

The Orlando metropolitan area population numbered 1.5 million in 2000. Today, Orlando has become the center of a future megalopolis stretching along Interstate 4 from Daytona to Tampa, the line of development roughly following the line of military forts established during the Second Seminole War.

Above: Hundreds of birds flock to Lake Eola each day to eat fish from the lake or to take advantage of the bread given out by the park's visitors.

PHOTO BY JOHN BRADLEY.

Below: The Central Florida Fair was one of the largest annual events in Orlando. It is still held today but on a much smaller scale.

COURTESY OF THE ORANGE COUNTY REGIONAL HISTORY CENTER.

Pine Castle

BY BARBARA KNOWLES

An aerial view of the Pinecastle Air Force Base taken on September 29, 1957.

COURTESY OF THE ORANGE COUNTY REGIONAL HISTORY CENTER.

There is nothing prettier than an orange grove in the night rain;
the flowers dashed with dew and the dark, glistening leaves new varnished in the moonlight.

- Will Wallace Harney
Pinecastle, Orange Co., Florida, September 15, 1875

Sitting in the grand English-style home he built and named "Pine Castle," author Will Wallace Harney wrote letters to the *Cincinnati Commercial* during the 1870s that transported its readers to the exotic land of orange groves, pine forests, and alligators. The heretofore unnamed area became Pine Castle when Harney changed his dateline from simply "Orange Co, FLA." to "Pinecastle." The 160-acre homestead was on the west side of Lake Conway, and the community that developed around it adopted the name.

Three hundred people lived in Pine Castle in the early 1920s, and some residents wanted it incorporated. Not everyone agreed, causing family and business arguments. To settle the problem, three separate towns were organized: Edgewood, Belle Isle, and Pine Castle. But when the real estate market crashed later in the decade, they had difficulty sustaining their tax bases. Pine Castle's government ended in 1929. With its charter dissolved, it became an unincorporated part of Orange County, which it remains today.

Walter C. Meloon moved to the Central Florida area in 1924, and the Florida Variety Boat Company was founded a year later. During World War II, the army asked the Meloons to build storm boats capable of crossing the treacherous Rhine River, Germany's last natural line of defense in the West. For a company that normally built 48 boats a month, the government's request for 300 boats in three weeks seemed impossible. Yet, the boat builders not only fulfilled the contract, but also made one hundred boats to spare. The Orlando-based business with worldwide operations, now called Correct Craft, operated from the same location until June 2006, when its need for expansion forced the company to move to East Orange County.

During World War II, the military needed to build an auxiliary field for the Orlando Army Air Field and began to clear land near Pine Castle. The Pinecastle Army Air Field became operational by 1943 and was used for research, development, and training by which pilots learned enemy technology and tactics that later helped to win the war. The base was deactivated in 1947 but reactivated as the Pinecastle Air Force Base in 1951 during the Korean War. On May 7, 1958 the base's name was changed to McCoy Air Force Base in honor of Colonel Michael McCoy, who was the 321st Bombardment Wing Commander at the base when his plane crashed near Orlando on October 9, 1957.

On October 14, 1962, Major Richard S. Heyser made a high-altitude reconnaissance flight over Cuba and photographed the Soviet military installing nuclear missiles, the action that triggered the Cuban Missile Crisis. The Air Force instructed Heyser to conclude his secretive flight at McCoy Air Force Base. During the two-week crisis, the Air Force continued to use McCoy for reconnaissance flights. The base was deactivated in 1975 and became the Orlando International Airport in 1981, but McCoy's legacy remains because officially it is still MCO to airlines and mail services.

Above: Downtown Pine Castle in the 1920s.

COURTESY OF THE ORANGE COUNTY REGIONAL HISTORY CENTER

Below: A plane at the Pinecastle Army Airfield.

COURTESY OF THE ORANGE COUNTY REGIONAL HISTORY CENTER

PINE HILLS

BY TANA MOSIER PORTER

Ken Curtis, best known for playing Festus Haggen on the CBS television series Gunsmoke, signed autographs for fans at the grand opening of the First National Bank at Pine Hills on April 1, 1960.

COURTESY OF THE ORANGE COUNTY REGIONAL HISTORY CENTER

Gordon Barnett established Pine Hills in 1952, beginning with six concrete block houses built along Pine Hills Road. When he bought the land on the northwest edge of the growing city of Orlando in 1945, more wildlife than people lived there. Colonial Drive came to a dead end at Tampa Avenue, but travelers who continued west on the Old Winter Garden Road eventually came to a rural settlement known as Robertsonville, named for Percy Robertson, head of the clan who occupied the cluster of houses. Barnett paid an average of $50 an acre for 2,200 acres of sand hills covered with pine and scrub oaks just north of Robertsonville.

Barnett bought the land as an investment at the beginning of Orange County's first postwar development boom. He planned to fill about forty acres of marsh and deep muck and build affordable housing for the working man, calling his development Orlando Hills. By the time the 9-hole golf course opened in 1947, Barnett had decided to call it Pine Hills instead. The highway department began surveying that year for a major road project, extending Highway 50 west from Orlando to Brooksville. The wider, straighter highway, which opened in 1949, made residential development possible outside the city limits, and Pine Hills became its first beneficiary.

Pine Hills had its formal opening on December 14, 1952, with paved streets and rows and rows of concrete block and brick houses. Barnett had completed 300 homes and planned to build more. The Pine Hills Drive-In Theater opened in June 1953 and a sundry shop in 1954. The Pine Hills Shopping Center started in 1956 with a Publix grocery store. With the Publix under construction, Barnett announced plans for a $2-million shopping center with thirty stores to open in 1958. By 1961, it had forty stores.

With new, affordable housing and convenient shopping not far from Orlando, Pine Hills occupied an enviable position in 1956 when the Glenn Martin Company, now Lockheed Martin, announced its plans to relocate to Orlando. The economic and physical growth that followed the company's arrival pushed the population of Pine Hills to more than 16,000 by 1970. Many of the first residents moved to Orange County with the Martin Company.

The Pine Hills Community Council, formed in the early 1970s, won Walt Disney World community service awards two years in a row, helped develop the Gordon Barnett Park, named for the founder of Pine Hills, and brought the Walsie L. Ward Girls Club to Pine Hills. As one of its projects in the 1970s, the Community Council moved to incorporate Pine Hills. An early attempt failed when most citizens stayed away from the meeting. In 1965, Pine Hills voted against both incorporation and annexation to Orlando and, in 1979, the Community Council's effort to incorporate failed.

In 1983 the 33,000 residents of Pine Hills lived on tree-lined residential streets in a neat geometric grid, five miles wide, between strip-zoned commercial highways on the north and south. The Pine Hills Merchants Association sponsored a Christmas parade and an annual sidewalk art festival. Residents blamed rapid growth for problems of perennial flooding and increasing crime. Residents formed neighborhood watch groups to contend with the crime wave that developed in the late 1970s.

According to the 2000 census, the population of 41,764 includes 51.4 percent African American, significantly higher than the state average, and 14.1 percent Hispanic, also above the state average. Residents find employment opportunities within the community in retail or in the light industry that surrounds Pine Hills. Pine Hills remains unincorporated, and residents still oppose annexation to Orlando.

Above: Residential area of Pine Hills can be seen in the background of this 1961 photograph.

COURTESY OF THE ORANGE COUNTY REGIONAL HISTORY CENTER

Below: Miss Pine Hills 1979 Laura Jenkins waves to the crowd at a local parade.

COURTESY OF THE ORANGE COUNTY REGIONAL HISTORY CENTER

TAFT

BY CASSANDRA FYOTEK

The Hotel Taft as it appeared in 1919.
COURTESY OF THE ORANGE COUNTY REGIONAL HISTORY CENTER.

Approximately eight miles south of Orlando lies the community of Taft. The area remained largely undeveloped until the South Florida Railroad passed through it in 1882, creating an easy mode of transportation for goods and people. The first known white settler to move to the area was Lester Newelton (Newlton) from Ashtabula, Ohio, in 1884. Naming the area Newelton, he hoped to use his land to grow citrus plants. However, his plan failed, and he sold off his land.

Although citrus was not originally successful, turpentine, lumber and farming proved otherwise in the early days of Taft. In 1900, Michael McKenzy Smith moved to the area and began a turpentine still and a turpentine camp. He renamed the community Smithville.

In 1905, Edward Lee, Dover Brooke, and William Govan Sphaler moved to Smithville. In addition to taking over Smith's turpentine still, the Sphaler Brothers also began operating a lumber mill and a shingle mill. A drought in 1906 damaged trees in the area, adversely affecting the lumber and shingle industries. The drought also took a toll on the cattle industry, encouraging people to take up farming instead. Fortunately for the small community, the Sphaler Brothers managed to remain successful.

In 1909, Braxton Beacham, along with W. L. Duzur, and Edward Lee Sphaler, established a farming community called Prosper Colony at the site of present-day Taft. Farms sold quickly thanks in large part to advertisements in such places as the *Saturday Evening Post*. The name of the settlement also changed to Taft, supposedly after President William Howard Taft.

The early success of Prosper Colony, however, did not last. Because of Taft's flat terrain, the area has always been prone to flooding after heavy storms. In 1910, a storm hit and flooded Prosper Colony. Although the storm ruined crops, forced settlers to leave, and doomed Prosper Colony, the town itself continued.

Despite the flood in 1910, Taft made some major developments in the first two decades of the twentieth century. In 1909, the town established a post office. In 1910, the town incorporated and built a train depot. In 1912, the first mayor, Nicholas Dennis, took office. In 1913, the town established the Taft Drainage District in order to help control flood waters and prevent a repeat of the Prosper Colony incident. In 1915, Dixie Highway, which runs through Taft, was bricked.

The Sphaler Brothers also played an important role in the developing community. They donated land for the first white school, which was built in 1910. The brothers also donated land for the First Baptist Church. The original structure burned down in 1912, only two years after it was built.

The African American community also made strides during this time. Reverend A. Williams established the first church in the area in 1902. The community also had the very first school in the area.

The late 1920s and 1930s brought hard times and challenges to the community. In 1926, a hurricane destroyed crops and homes. In 1929, the stock market crashed and the Great Depression of the 1930s hit small communities such as Taft especially hard. In 1935, there was another damaging hurricane.

Although the previous decades were tough, after World War II, Taft saw further development. Pinecastle Army Airfield, later Orlando International Airport, brought new people and businesses to the area. Industrial Parks for UPS, FedEx, and ABC Liquors emerged, and the CX Railroad expanded. The citizens of Taft also had a hand in developing their community. Their efforts led to a community center, a volunteer fire department, although Orange County firemen later replaced them, and a neighborhood watch association.

Taft's history is rich with a sense of community pride. Today's citizens of Taft are no different. With community programs they have been fighting to reduce crime and drugs and to create a brighter future for the small town just south of Orlando.

In 1909, Braxton Beacham, seated at right, helped to establish a farming community called Prosper Colony on the present day site of Taft. Beacham also served as Mayor of Orlando in 1907.

COURTESY OF THE ORANGE COUNTY REGIONAL HISTORY CENTER

A 1918 advertisement for Dr. B. Lust's Health Resort in Tangerine, Florida.

COURTESY OF THE ORANGE COUNTY REGIONAL HISTORY CENTER.

TANGERINE

BY TANA MOSIER PORTER

Escaping bronchial trouble, Dudley W. Adams, of Iowa, located on Lake Beauclair in northwest Orange County in 1875. He built a log cabin and later a permanent home. Brothers Lewis and Henry Marot arrived in 1878 and started a store. Raymond J. Wright, came from Michigan in search of health in 1878. J. E. Manley and Holland Williams came in the 1870s. Other early settlers included Dr. Hedge, William Russ, David Simpson, O. J. Bean, J. W. Kelley, Colonel Gaines, H. J. Foster, and W. E. Hudson.

A village developed around the Adams house on the Ocklawaha chain of lakes in the ridges of Florida's citrus belt. On Lake Beauclaire, with Lake Dora to the north and Lakes Carlton and Ola to the south, the town became Olaville, for the lake, reportedly named to honor an Indian chief's beautiful daughter, Ola. As the village grew into a town, Miss Bessie Heustis, sister-in-law of Adams, suggested changing the name to Tangerine for the tangerine tree growing near her doorstep. The citizens met in her log cabin in 1879 and voted to change the name of the settlement from Olaville to Tangerine.

Tangerine pioneers cleared the land and planted citrus groves. By 1885, Dudley Adams cultivated 3,000 trees, Raymond Wright had 2,000, William Terry 2,500, and Dr. Hedge 500 trees. Adams' sister-in-law, Miss B. Huestis, maintained five hundred trees. In addition to citrus, early nurseries experimented with shipping cut flowers to florists in the 1880s. James Mott, whose nursery also included as many as 100,000 orange trees, began shipping peaches north in 1889.

Some supplies came by oxcart, but after Tangerine built a dock on Lake Beauclaire, produce going north crossed the lake by steamer to Tavares to be loaded on the Tavares & Gulf Railroad. Citizens refused to allow either the Seaboard Air Line or the Atlantic Coastline Railroads to lay tracks through Tangerine, arguing that they wanted a select community of homes.

The Tangerine Development Society, organized in 1880, governed the town. A post office opened in Tangerine in 1881, when the community counted fifty residents.

Tangerine had a school from 1881 until 1944, beginning with a log cabin on Lake Ola and the first teacher, Miss Minnie Wright. The town built a school building in 1886. The Congregational Church organized in 1886 and built a building in 1888 that stood for many years as the Tangerine Community Church. By 1885, as many as 250 people received mail at the Tangerine post office.

Several African American families settled to the north and east of the village center early in Tangerine's history. The Stalling brothers, Felix and Wes, brought their families in the 1870s, and the Woodbury brothers, Wiley, Richard, Louis, Archie, their sister and their parents followed in the 1880s. The settlement grew to support two churches and a one-room school for the black children. Known as Tangerine Black, it became part of the county school system in 1886 and remained open until 1966.

The Acme Hotel, Tangerine's first, opened in 1883. It became the Wauchusett House in 1884, and later the Lake Ola Lodge. In 1914, Dr. Benedict Lust of New York, opened his second naturopathic health resort in the former hotel. Lust's original Yungborn resort opened in 1896, in Butler, New Jersey, as a summer resort, and the Tangerine Yungborn, also called Qui-Si-Sana, operated only during the winter. Dr. Lust, a well-known naturopath, treated patients with regeneration cures based on diet, exercise, fresh air, and sunshine. Dr. Lust died in 1945, and the clinic burned during the early 1940s.

The Tangerine Improvement Society, organized in 1909 for "the interests and advancement of the community," raised money in 1911 for a town hall, officially named Tangerine Hall. The Improvement Society established Tangerine Park in 1937 "as a public park for young and old forever." Tangerine remains unincorporated. The 2000 population of 826 included 87 percent white non-Hispanic, 8 percent Hispanic, and 3 percent black.

The community grew slowly for many years; the population increased to 830 in 1990, then declined to 826 in 2000. But growth and development surround Tangerine and threaten the rural way of life. Tangerine and Mount Dora opposed plans to develop land nearby in 1994, and won a delay from Orange County. In 2000, Tangerine residents protested plans for a massive development and negotiated a compromise on the plans, but in 2004 new proposals promised more developments.

DR. B. LUST'S **RECREATION RESORT for NATURE AND LIFE**

FLORIDA "YUNGBORN"

MOUNT DORA on Atlantic Coast Line **"QUI-SI-SANA," TANGERINE, FLA.** **ZELLWOOD** on Seaboard Air Line

Natural Life and Rational Cure Health Home for Dietetic-Physical-Atmospheric Regeneration Treatment. Fount of Youth, and New Life School for those in need of Cure and Rest, for the physically and spiritually weakened, for those overworked, and for the convalescent.

OPEN ALL THE YEAR

IN the vicinity of the most beautiful lakes in Florida, and country town of Mount Dora, there spreads, in incomparably ideal beauty, surrounded by majestic pine forests, orchards and parks, the Health Resort of YUNGBORN (born young again), "QUISISANA" (place where you get Health). The establishment was called *Yungborn* by reason of the rejuvenating and strength-endowing effects of its Regeneration Cures; and, indeed, these extensively known Yungborn-Regeneration Cures are not only health-restoring, but also Rejuvenating and Strength-giving Cures. Already during, and particularly after the treatments are completed, the strength and vitality, formerly low and broken, rise with astonishing assurance. Vital energy and vital strength return; increased nerve-elasticity and an undreamed-of sensation of powerful health make themselves felt, and with the new creative power, there asserts itself a feeling of spiritual and physical rejuvenation and unlimited efficiency in the human system.

Orange and Palm trees in the Florida "Yungborn"

Yungborn Regeneration Cures—The dietetical Regeneration Cures which are applied in their particular gradations as required for the various diseases and conditions of weakness, are fully adapted to the case in hand and modified correspondingly.

The most peculiar and most intense forms of these Cures are the *Schroth Treatment*, so called after its founder, the genial Johann Schroth, and the combined *Diet, Light-Air and Water Treatments* in which the experiences of *Kuhne, Kneipp, Rickli, Lahmann, Ehret, Just, Engelhardt*, etc., are resorted to individually. Furthermore, Fruit Cures, Herb Cures Vegetal and Mixed Diet, Fasting, Diet Cures in combination with Fruit Diets, and so forth, are employed. Diet requires adapted physical treatment, such as *packings*, bandaging, baths and gushes of various descriptions, barefoot walking, light *sun* and *air baths*, steam, electricity, massaging, and Osteopathy, Chiropractic, Mechanotherapy, Neuropathy, etc. Special attention is given to the development of humid warmth treatment—one of the most important curative factors.

Boating on beautiful Lake Ola

Aid in Obsolete, Inveterate Cases—The Yungborn Regeneration Cures will help even in the most deep-seated superannuated conditions of suffering and weakness, where other cures failed, except in cases of organic new growth and destructions (like cancer and consumption) or marasmus. It need hardly be mentioned that not only those requiring cure, but also *those in need of rest—the weakened and convalescing*—derive the best possible benefits of lasting effect from a sojourn at the Yungborn—home of health.

In 1927, Qui-Si-Sana, known at that time as Naturpath Sanitarium, was considered one of the best health resorts in Florida.

COURTESY OF THE ORANGE COUNTY REGIONAL HISTORY CENTER

Windermere

BY CYNTHIA CARDONA MELÉNDEZ

A typical camp along Lake Butler.

COURTESY OF THE ORANGE COUNTY REGIONAL HISTORY CENTER.

Nestled on an isthmus among three spring-like lakes is the small town of Windermere, dubbed at one time, the place to live for "health and wealth for all who seek." Like several other communities in Orange County, Windermere's early settlers were from England, one of whom was Florida Midland Railroad employee John H. Dawe. In 1887, Dawe laid out the town and named it after the lake town in England. Other British settlers followed, most notably Dr. Stanley Scott, who had 160 acres purchased for him by his father on the west side of Lake Butler. Scott named the land Kelso Groves and began growing citrus, ushering in Orange County's burgeoning citrus industry to Windermere.

In 1888, brothers Joshua and Sydney Chase of Pennsylvania purchased forty-six acres of land in Windermere in order to plant citrus, naming the land Isleworth. This land was a small island located in Lake Butler, making its proximity to warm water prime for citrus growing due in part to the protection the warm water provided against freezes. Prior to purchasing this key piece of land, Sydney Chase worked for Henry Sanford, founder of Sanford, Florida, in Seminole County. Chase worked on Sanford's Belair citrus grove where he quickly obtained valuable knowledge about the citrus industry. The Chase's initial land purchase eventually grew to include close to seven hundred acres of grove land, making the Chases one of Orange County's largest and most successful citrus-growing dynasties.

Windermere's idealistic setting on the headwaters of the Butler Chain of Lakes also attracted fishermen and the keen eyes of Ohioans John Calvin Palmer and Dr. J. Howard Johnson, who created the Windermere Improvement Company in 1911 in order to promote investment in the small town, sell plots of land, and to tout the area's growing citrus industry to wealthy northerners.

Left: Residents of Windermere enjoy a fish fry on Lake Down in 1909.
COURTESY OF THE ORANGE COUNTY REGIONAL HISTORY CENTER

Below: The 1890 Windermere School, also known as the Armstrong-Parramore House, is listed on the National Register of Historic Places.
PHOTO BY JOHN BRADLEY

Bottom: The Pine Tree Inn was built in 1914 by Dr. and Mrs. J. A. Thompson of Cleveland, Ohio. It was destroyed by fire in 1937.
COURTESY OF THE ORANGE COUNTY REGIONAL HISTORY CENTER

By 1920, the success of the promotional efforts of the Windermere Improvement Company were evident as the town boasted a public school, a church, two general stores, and the near completion of an asphalt road.

The accelerated growth witnessed by other parts of Orange County in the early twentieth century did not affect Windermere, and the small community was able to keep growth and population surges to a minimum, with its population not exceeding one thousand people until the 1980s. In 1983, The Chase Company sold all of its Isleworth property to a group of investors led by golf legend Arnold Palmer. Palmer and his team developed an upscale community around one of his signature golf courses, making Isleworth a premier place to live for the extremely wealthy. Today, Windermere and its famed Isleworth community, is home to many sports figures, notably golfer Tiger Woods and former Orlando Magic player Shaquille O'Neil.

WINTER GARDEN

BY TANA MOSIER PORTER

Winter Garden's first Strawberry Festival was held in 1926. R. P. Howard, right, and Smith Blair drove this float from Winter Garden to Lake Eola in downtown Orlando to advertise the festival.

COURTESY OF THE ORANGE COUNTY REGIONAL HISTORY CENTER.

The largest community in the south Lake Apopka region of West Orange County, settled in the 1850s, became known as Winter Garden in the early 1900s. The first settlers included the Harrell, Singer, B. B. Reams, and A. J. Dunaway families. W. C. Roper moved his family from Georgia in 1860 in a caravan made up of twenty-eight horses and mules, five wagons, two carriages, and one buggy. Judge J.G. Speer arrived about 1857, as did J. D. Starke and Colonel Isaac Hudson. J. L. Dillard came from Virginia in 1887, and later pioneered in the use of rough lemon root stock in cultivating citrus.

Some of the first settlers went to nearby Beulah, and then moved on to what became Winter Garden. They found the land suitable for corn, cotton, sugar cane, and sweet potatoes. Cotton became an important money maker, while the other crops provided for family needs. Everyone living on the scattered farms and homesteads kept hogs in the woods and cattle on the range. The warm climate, fertile and adaptable soil, good water, and the moderate temperatures along Lake Apopka made the area ideal for citrus groves. Captain B. M. Sims started the first known citrus grove in nearby Ocoee in 1865.

The first growers shipped cotton and other crops by steamer down the St. Johns River to Jacksonville, barging them on the Wekiva River from Clay Springs to the St. Johns or hauling them by ox-drawn wagon to Sanford. By the 1880s, growers shipped tomatoes, cucumbers, and citrus fruit to northern markets by rail, from their own depot after 1893. The Orange Belt Railroad, opened in 1888, brought significant growth to Winter Garden. The tracks ran through the center of the downtown, dividing Plant Street, Winter Garden's main corridor. The Tavares & Gulf Railroad reached Clermont by 1887 and moved on toward Winter Garden in 1899. The Orange Belt Railroad became part of the Plant System in 1902.

A post office opened in Winter Garden in 1892, despite protests from post offices in neighboring Ocoee and Oakland. The Great Freeze of 1894-1895 devastated many of the places that were so heavily dependent on citrus cultivation, but Winter Garden turned to truck farming and continued to maintain a dual agricultural economy as the groves came back to production. Catfish from Lake Apopka, crated and shipped north, provided another cash crop in the early 1900s. The Winter Garden Citrus Growers Association and South Lake Apopka Citrus Growers Association cooperatives organized in 1909 to give independent growers the advantages of joint ownership in shipping, harvesting, marketing, and bulk purchases of fertilizer and chemicals. The Florida Citrus Exchange formed the same year to help regulate freight rates and sales in the increasingly prosperous citrus market.

In 1900, the population stood at approximately one hundred, and the small commercial district along Plant and Main Streets included two hotels. Winter Garden incorporated in 1908 with nearly two hundred residents. The origin of the name and the date of its first use remain uncertain. Several people seem to have suggested calling the place Winter Garden, including the group of growers who built the first railroad depot in 1893 and who needed a name for the stop on the Orange Belt Railroad.

Above: A. B. Newton established Winter Garden's first orange packing house. Newton was a pioneer businessman and served in many capacities within the city's government.

COURTESY OF THE ORANGE COUNTY REGIONAL HISTORY CENTER.

The town began providing municipal services such as water and sewers between 1900 and 1910. A telephone exchange went into operation in 1908, the same year the Bank of Winter Garden opened. The first residential subdivision, Millers Plat of Winter Garden, opened in 1907, followed by as many as fourteen smaller subdivisions before World War I. These included Loveless' Addition for African Americans, platted at Center and Ninth Streets in 1910. Winter Garden had 351 residents by 1910, and three churches and nearly fifty buildings by World War I.

The first permanent brick buildings went up in 1912 on Plant Street, after a fire destroyed

Below: Britt's Lettuce Farm, as seen on January 2, 1922, covered 400 acres of land in Winter Garden.

COURTESY OF THE ORANGE COUNTY REGIONAL HISTORY CENTER.

Above: Lakeview High School operated from 1927 to its closing in 1975 when it combined with Ocoee High School to form West Orange High School. The building now serves as Lakeview Middle School.
COURTESY OF THE ORANGE COUNTY REGIONAL HISTORY CENTER.

Below: According to a 1939 issue of Orange Echoes, *Trailer City was "one of the most beautiful, modern and comfortable trailer parks in the United States."*
COURTESY OF THE ORANGE COUNTY REGIONAL HISTORY CENTER.

the downtown business district in 1909. The Winter Garden Theater opened in 1913. The Tavares & Gulf Railroad built a new station in 1913, on the site of one from 1899, and the Atlantic Coastline Railroad replaced its depot with a new one in 1918.

The first paved highway, a nine-foot-wide brick road came from Oakland, through Winter Garden, and on to Orlando in 1915. Hoyle Pounds opened a garage in Ocoee in 1914, and then moved his Pounds Motor Company to Winter Garden in 1920. An inventor, Pounds developed rubber tires for tractors, a tree cultivator, and a fertilizer distributor.

Developers platted 19 subdivisions and built more than 300 new buildings between 1920 and 1930 during the Florida Land Boom. Winter Garden's population increased from 1,021 in 1920 to 2,023 by 1930, and the old school, built in 1919 and expanded in 1924, could not accommodate the students. The new Lakeview High School opened in 1927. Winter Garden boasted four miles of brick-paved roads in 1924, and reincorporated as a city in 1925, with A. B. Newton as its first mayor. The fifty-two-room Edgewater Hotel opened in 1927.

Historically, citrus provided the main cash crop. Winter Garden shipped twenty-five hundred rail cars of citrus and vegetables in 1925, and the continuing demand for citrus products mitigated the effects of the Great Depression of the 1930s, though Winter Garden's economy suffered in 1929 and 1930, and the Winter Garden Bank closed in 1929. In a citrus economy, the discovery of the Mediterranean fruit fly in 1929 did more damage than the Depression, as government inspectors quarantined groves and stationed armed guards to prevent shipment of the diseased fruit.

The Federal Works Progress Administration helped finance a twelve-acre tourist camp along Lake Apopka in the 1930s. Called Trailer City, it included an auditorium, boat basins and a dock, a swimming pool, and a bathhouse. In 1940, Winter Garden counted 3,060 residents and seven citrus-packing houses. The Roper Brothers, who had incorporated in 1931, established a juice

Left: Downtown Winter Garden in the 1920s.

COURTESY OF THE ORANGE COUNTY REGIONAL HISTORY CENTER

packing plant in 1944 to meet the great demand for canned juice during World War II. In April 1950 the Winter Garden Citrus Products Cooperative began manufacturing frozen juice concentrate.

In the late 1940s developers platted eight new subdivisions around Winter Garden to accommodate expanding residential neighborhoods, but the agricultural economy and the absence of major highways passing through town moderated the growth of Winter Garden itself. The downtown remained little changed until the early 1950s, when the completion of Highway 50 several miles south of Winter Garden drew business away from Main Street.

The downtown declined in the 1960s, and many of the old commercial buildings disappeared. Few buildings remained by 1990 of the nearly 150 built by the end of World War II, raising concerns about the loss of cultural heritage. The Winter Garden Heritage Foundation organized to pursue private support for revitalizing the historic community. Main Street Winter Garden formed, and the old Atlantic Coastline tracks through town became a park, part of the West Orange Trail. The community restored the Garden Theater and the 1927 Edgewater Hotel.

Winter Garden's population grew from 5,093 in 1960 to 5,513 in 1970. After Walt Disney World opened in 1971, the population increased, to 6,789 in 1980 and 10,186 in 1990, but fewer residents worked in Winter Garden. The 2000 population of 14,351 included 67 percent Caucasian, 13 percent African American, and 18 percent Hispanic.

Below: Roper Brothers began in 1918. In addition to "Boss," Roper Brothers also marketed their citrus under the brands "Ship Ahoy" and "Full Ahead."

COURTESY OF THE ORANGE COUNTY REGIONAL HISTORY CENTER

Winter Park

BY STEPHANIE GAUB

An aerial view of Winter Park showing Lakes Maitland and Osceola.

COURTESY OF THE ORANGE COUNTY REGIONAL HISTORY CENTER.

"The whole State of Florida is challenged to produce a prettier or healthier spot. Look everywhere, but be sure and see Winter Park before locating" professed an 1888 Winter Park promotional booklet. Now home to some of the area's most affluent citizens and the prestigious shops of Park Avenue, Winter Park traces its roots to New Englanders traveling south for health reasons.

Winter Park's first resident, David Mizell, moved his family to the scrubland of the Winter Park area in 1858. He called his new settlement Lake View and built a log cabin near present day Phelps and Mizell avenues, eventually growing enough cotton, livestock, and vegetables to sustain himself, his wife, and their ten children. The Mizells had few neighbors until Chicagoan Loring Chase and his friend Oliver Chapman realized the potential the area had for winter homes and health tourism.

Loring Chase suffered from chronic bronchitis and, at the urging of his physician, came to Florida in February 1881 for the climate's celebrated health benefits. "A residence of a few months in the pine woods a few miles west of where Winter Park now stands, completely cured him. His headaches and cough left him, and he was quite naturally filled with enthusiasm for the climate." During his stay in Orange County, Chase traveled extensively throughout the area but kept coming back to an area covered with beautiful high-rolling land, magnificent pines, and over two miles of sparkling lakes. He convinced Chapman to visit the land that he raved about and, on July 1, 1881, the two men purchased 600 acres of land for $13,000 and proceeded to survey and plot the town they named Winter Park. In their planning, they allowed for a central park bisected by a central boulevard and three lakefront sites for resort hotels.

New residents and visitors touted the health benefits of Winter Park. Newspapers across the country carried word of the disease-free town as well as testimonials by the many individuals who experienced these benefits first hand.

> Asthma finds a certain relief here. Ask H. S. Kedney, who has suffered from boyhood, and who, after seeking relief in all parts of the world, came here, and was cured.
>
> Hay-fever is cured here. Ask Dr. E. Martin, who was terribly afflicted when he came, and was cured in a short time.
>
> Children are remarkably healthy here. Diphtheria and croup are unknown.
>
> Catarrh finds here a sure and speedy relief. Ask L. A. Chase of Winter Park, who came here from Chicago in 1881 with one of the worst possible cases."

Consumption, pulmonary hemorrhages, chronic diseases of the mucous membranes, kidney troubles, and rheumatic afflictions were all said to be healed by the climate of Winter Park. One doctor even went so far as to declare Winter Park as "the healthiest spot on the face of the globe."

Loring Chase added to the allure of Winter Park by talking-up the new town to wealthy northerners during his many trips to Jacksonville, Florida. Between 1881 and 1885, the two men continued to advertise the fledgling town. They also opened additional streets, planted orange trees, and built a store, town hall, and cottages. Many prominent residents, including Charles Hosmer Morse, Colonel Franklin Fairbanks, and Francis B. Knowles, bought land in Winter Park during this time, and the small town won the legislative fight for Florida's first four-year college.

Morse came to Winter Park in the winter of 1881-82. He spent many winters in the town, garnering a deep involvement in the community in 1904 when he took possession of the Knowles estate and gained control of the Winter Park Company, the organization which allowed for promotion and development of the town. The estate transfer made Morse the largest land-holder in Winter Park. Morse's legacy lives on in Winter Park as the city hall, golf course, Woman's Club, and Central Park are each located on land donated by Morse. In addition, Morse's granddaughter founded a museum in 1942 that houses the world's largest collection of works by Louis Comfort Tiffany and named it The Charles Hosmer Morse Museum of American Art.

Fairbanks came to Winter Park with his friend and business associate Morse in 1881. He purchased a lot on Interlachen Avenue facing Lake Osceola and became vice president of The Winter Park Company, an original stockholder in the Seminole Hotel, and a charter trustee of Rollins College. Today, Fairbanks Avenue bears his name.

Above: Looking at the photograph of Winter Park in 1883, it is hard to imagine Chase and Campbell successfully marketing the town to northerners.

COURTESY OF THE ORANGE COUNTY REGIONAL HISTORY CENTER

Below: New England Avenue is unrecognizable in this 1885 photograph.

COURTESY OF THE ORANGE COUNTY REGIONAL HISTORY CENTER

Above: Downtown Winter Park, April 28, 1925.

COURTESY OF THE ORANGE COUNTY REGIONAL HISTORY CENTER

Below: An early nineteenth century postcard showing one of the many picturesque lakes in Winter Park.

COURTESY OF THE ORANGE COUNTY REGIONAL HISTORY CENTER

Francis B. Knowles made his first trip to Florida in 1883 and happened upon his old friend Franklin Fairbanks. After learning of the wonders of Winter Park, Knowles finally moved to the town in 1885. He became a director of The Winter Park Company as well as its largest stockholder. Knowles helped found Rollins College, served as a member of its first Board of Trustees, and financed the college's first building, Knowles Hall. Knowles also enabled the completion of the Orlando and Winter Park Railroad, commonly known as the "Dinky Line," and gave funds for the construction of Knowles Public School. "Mr. Knowles bore his prosperity modestly. The great bulk of his income has been dispensed to charities of which the public never had an inkling and he chose that they should not."

From its inception, the town plan allowed for "Negro Lots…west of [the] railroad in Hannibal Square…." African Americans in Winter Park tended to work as servants in the homes of the town's wealthy residents or to hold positions with the railroad. African Americans in Winter Park held town positions as early as 1887 when it chose Walter B. Simpson and Frank R. Israel to serve as aldermen even though blacks did not have voting privileges and the South remained segregated until the 1960s. Even the town's newspaper, The *Winter Park Advocate*, was located in Hannibal Square and run by a highly respected black editor, Gus Henderson. The newspaper covered news for both the white and black communities.

Edwin O. Grover, Royal W. France, Eulalie O. Grover, W. E. Winderweedle, and J. L. Houston formed the not-for-profit corporation of Hannibal Square Associates, Inc., in 1937. The articles of incorporation stated:

> The general nature of the object of this corporation shall be: to establish, own and operate a public library; to own and develop a recreation center and any other enterprise for the social and civic betterment of the Negro population of Winter Park, Florida; and to promote and encourage education and the attendance of the Negro population of the City of Winter Park at institutions of higher learning; to cultivate the artistic, scientific and literary tastes and aspirations of the Negro population of the City of Winter Park.

Despite all of its success, Hannibal Square Associates ceased to exist on June 9, 1968. The Hannibal Square Library Branch became part of the Hannibal Square Neighborhood Service Center. The library closed in 1979 when the new Winter Park Public Library opened.

As a result of all of this, Hannibal Square earned a reputation as one of the strongest and most resourceful black communities in the state. More recently, Hannibal Square has become home to some of Winter Park's more illustrious dining and shopping establishments despite opposition from those who live in the area. In 2007, the Crealdé School of Art created the Hannibal Square Heritage Center which houses an exhibit on the history of the community as told by its residents.

In 1885, five communities competed for the privilege of playing host to Florida's first four-year college. The Congregational Church wanted to create an institution of higher learning in Florida to rival the best schools in New England. Daytona Beach, Mount Dora, Orange City, Jacksonville, and Winter Park each submitted proposals at the Congregational Association's meeting in Mount Dora.

> Mount Dora offered a 10-acre wooded site on Lake Dora, cash, lumber and another 700 acres for a total value of $35,564.... Daytona Beach anteed up $20,000 and an oceanfront location. Jacksonville offered only $13,000 and land for the college campus. Orange City made a modest proposal of $10,000...."

Frederick Wolcott Lyman stunned the competitors when he announced Winter Park's offer of $125,000, made possible in large part by a $50,000 pledge from Chicago businessman Alonzo Rollins. Three days later, the association unanimously voted to build the college in Winter Park and to name it after Rollins.

The school kept the tuition low to attract students. The first classroom building opened in March 1886, followed soon by men's and women's dormitories and a dining hall. By 1888, Rollins College had three departments, the course of study in each occupying four years. The school promoted itself by declaring that:

> ...young ladies and gentlemen who cannot endure the Northern winters, and yet have health sufficient to pursue their studies under favorable circumstances, will find here an institution of the best grade, and in a delightful climate, where they may hope to pass safely their most critical years, and go forth with health confirmed to strong and useful lives.

Above: Students at Rollins College perform The Merchant of Venice *in 1903.*

COURTESY OF THE ORANGE COUNTY REGIONAL HISTORY CENTER

Below: Female students gather outside of Corrin Hall on the campus of Rollins College, c. 1946.

COURTESY OF THE ORANGE COUNTY REGIONAL HISTORY CENTER

In May 1890, Rollins celebrated its first commencement with the graduation of Clara Louise Guild and Ida May Misseldine. Rollins continues to receive national accolades for its dedication to providing a quality liberal arts education.

Residents of Winter Park had additional cause for jubilation in 1885 with the construction of the Seminole Hotel. Located on the banks of Lake Osceola, the Seminole Hotel boasted five floors with rooms for 400 guests, making it the largest hotel south of Jacksonville, Florida. The hotel opened on New Year's Day 1886, and consisted of the most modern amenities: steam heat, gas lighting, an elevator, fire alarm system, and steam baths. The dining tables offered "...milk, poultry, eggs, vegetables, oranges, guavas, and other fruits, from farms near by [sic], and the best of meats from Northern markets." Guests could partake of bowling, billiards, croquet, tennis, or bathing or rowing on the lakes. In its first year of operation, the Seminole Hotel became so popular that it had to turn away guests. Tragedy struck the Seminole Hotel on September 17, 1902, when it burned to the ground.

Chase and Campbell's dreams continue to flourish in the Winter Park of today, and many of the opulent homes built in the late nineteenth century still stand as a reminder of the residents who saw beauty and promise in the small town.

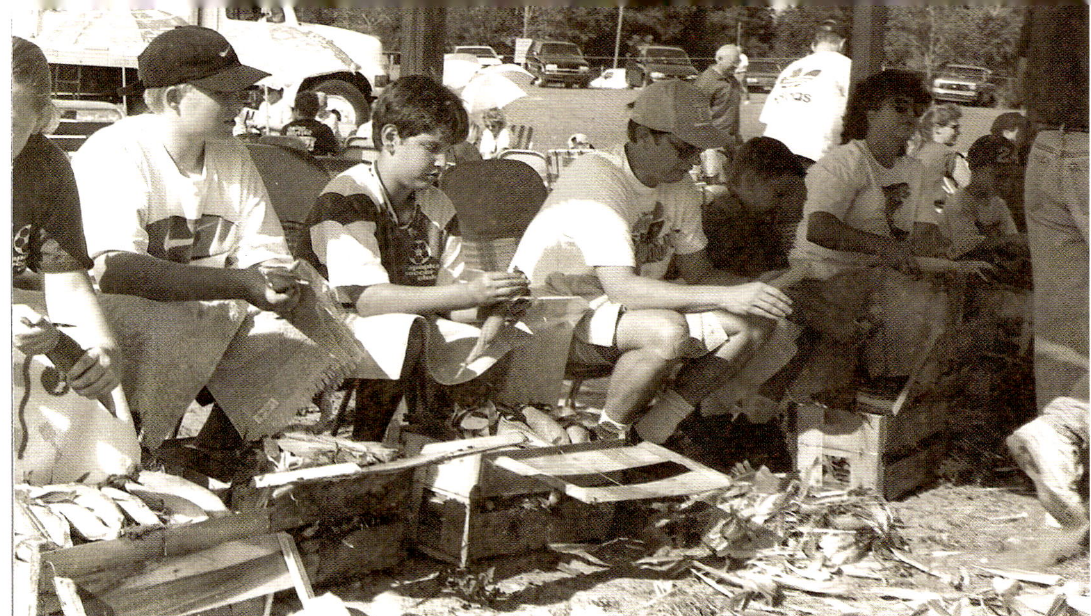

Zellwood

BY GARRET KREMER-WRIGHT

The Zellwood Sweet Corn Festival features "Big Bertha," a 350-gallon kettle that cooks 1,650 ears of corn every nine minutes.

COURTESY OF THE ORANGE COUNTY REGIONAL HISTORY CENTER.

Nestled among lakes, rolling hills, and citrus groves in northern Orange County lies the small community of Zellwood. The town is located a few miles north of Apopka. The name Zellwood is derived from one of its earliest settlers, Colonel T. Elwood Zell. He came to the area from Philadelphia in 1876 and made it his winter home. Other early settlers to the area were John A. Williamson and James Laughlin, Jr. Williamson's house became the center of social activity during this time because of the immense size of it. It was not uncommon for him to host dances, religious activities, and theatrical performances. Potential new settlers would also stay in the house while they were looking for land to buy. Laughlin came to Zellwood from Pittsburgh between 1882 and 1883. He proceeded to build his estate called Sydonie (completed in 1904) on the banks of Lake Maggiore. He would later become a trustee and benefactor of Rollins College.

During the 1880s, the town began to grow, with numerous families moving into the area. This is evident by the number of public facilities that opened during this time. The first school began in 1877, followed soon after by the opening of the library in 1888. The Tavares, Orlando, Atlantic Railroad came through in 1883, and the station depot was completed in 1885. Highway improvements came to the area during World War I when Highway 441 came through. It was expanded to four lanes in 1943.

Zellwood is known most for its muck lands. The fifteen-thousand-acre area is situated around Lake Apopka. The marshlands were drained around the lake in 1909, and they first planted Irish potatoes. However, the potatoes soon rotted when water flooded the region. In 1920 Richard Whitney founded the Florida (Zellwood) Humus Co. This company scooped up the wet mud and let it dry in the sun and then sold it in bulk. The fern industry came to the area in 1922 when the Fern Growers' Association was organized. Today, World Foliage Resource, Inc., has their main plant in Zellwood. The Zellwood Drainage and Water Control District was established in 1941 by the Florida legislature to help control the area. Soon after this establishment came farmers who planted a variety of vegetables that thrived on the nutrients that the muck provided. The most common vegetables grown were corn and carrots. Unfortunately the draining of the lake and subsequent discharge of fertilizer from surrounding farms caused it to become polluted. The state bought out the land for almost $91 million in 1998 with the hope of trying to restore the lake to its once pristine beauty. Nearly two thousand farmers lost their jobs overnight.

Zellwood is home to the annual Sweet Corn Festival. What became a festival began in 1968 as a community corn boil that included Kentucky Fried Chicken. In 1973 the first official festival drew 12,800 people. That number grew to thirty thousand in 2006. After all the people leave though, the residents settle down and realize just why they came to live in this quiet little town they call home.

Select-O-Sweet Brand was marketed by Zellwood Fruit Distributors.

COURTESY OF THE ORANGE COUNTY REGIONAL HISTORY CENTER

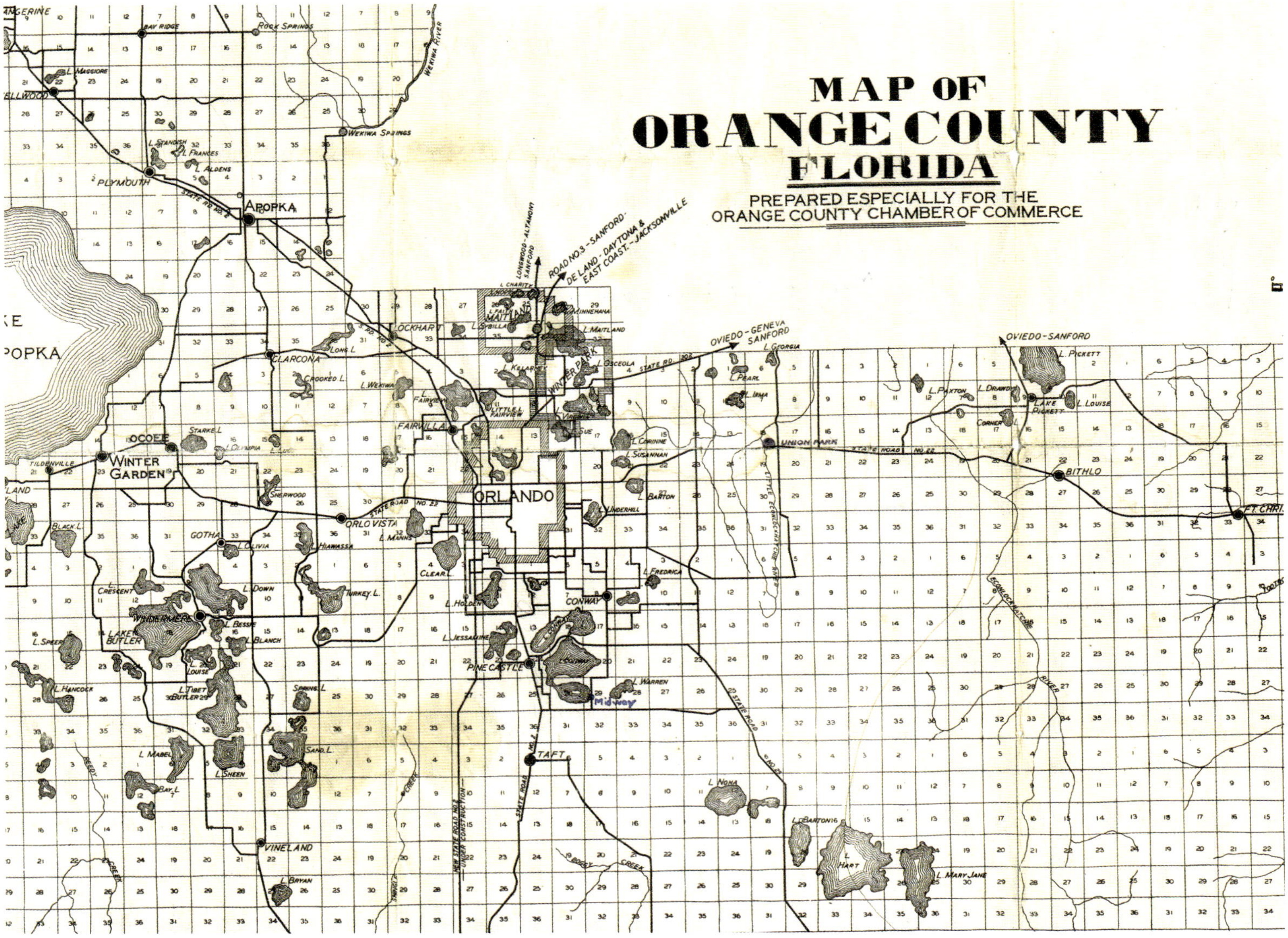

Vanishing Communities

BY BARBARA KNOWLES

A map of Orange County, c. 1930, showing the many small communities found across the county.

COURTESY OF THE ORANGE COUNTY REGIONAL HISTORY CENTER.

The expansion of the railroad through Orange County during the 1880s brought settlers eager to make their homes in Florida's warm climate. The resulting population boom transformed the county's landscape as settlements and towns formed along waterways and railroad tracks.

Due to limited modes of transportation and communication, many of these communities developed only a mile or two apart, each with its own basic needs. Today, a city requires a hospital, and a police and fire station. But, in Orange County's pioneer days, a town needed at most a sawmill and maybe a general store.

The Big Freeze of the mid-1890s was an economic deathblow for many communities. And, as transportation and communication improved in the twentieth century, towns with better locations or other advantages became the economic hubs of the region. Some towns disappeared without a trace, while others are identifiable today primarily by their road signs or their subdivision names.

Following is a look at some of these communities, all of which are part of Central Florida's rich history.

BAY RIDGE

Founded primarily by New Englanders between 1885 and 1886, Bay Ridge was about three miles northeast of Zellwood. Settlers skilled in carpentry, plaster work, and cistern building contributed to Bay Ridge's growth. Jacob and Jessie Anderson owned the town's sawmill, which was a half mile northwest of the store and post office. Sometime after 1912, the sawmill burned, and Bay Ridge did not recover.

BEULAH

Beulah was one of the region's oldest communities, founded sometime before the Civil War and located three miles south of Winter Garden. After he was discharged from the army in 1865, Captain B. M. Sims, who was originally from Tennessee, moved to Beulah and taught school for several terms in the area's first schoolhouse. He also was the contractor for Orlando's first framed courthouse, which was constructed with lumber sawed and planed in Beulah. By the mid-1920s, the community was no longer on the map, possibly because of the economic downturn of the area prior to the Great Depression.

CLARCONA

William Clark of Lakeville purchased several hundred acres of pristine land south of Apopka in the 1880s and erected a sawmill. This area in the thick backwoods began to be referred to as Clark's Corner. Through repeated usage, probably helped along by residents' country accents, the name evolved into one word, Clarcona.

It had a few settlers among its rolling hills and lakes—all of which was conducive to growing citrus. In the 1980s, Clarcona residents, wanting to retain their rural identity, organized in an attempt to block urban development. Although their efforts appeared to slow down growth in the area, all that remains today of Clarcona is a community center, a post office, and a couple of convenience stores.

CLAY SPRINGS

Today, Wekiwa Springs is a state park, but originally the town, which was called Clay Springs until 1906, competed with Apopka to be the political center of the area. A few residents lived in Clay Springs before the Civil War. There was a wharf and a warehouse, but the little town couldn't rival Apopka's more established location for business.

During the 1880s, many communities started from the vision of a single individual. J. D. Smith, an Iowa newspaperman, bought property and laid out a town less than a mile from Clay Springs. He named it Sulphur Springs after the sulphur-producing spring

Above: Jacob W. Anderson's sawmill, c. 1889.

COURTESY OF THE ORANGE COUNTY REGIONAL HISTORY CENTER

Below: The 1875 Orange County Courthouse was built with wood from Beulah.

COURTESY OF THE ORANGE COUNTY REGIONAL HISTORY CENTER

Above: *A toboggan slide and pavilion at Clay Springs.*

COURTESY OF THE ORANGE COUNTY REGIONAL HISTORY CENTER.

Below: Residents of Grasmere enjoy a day at Clay Springs.

COURTESY OF THE ORANGE COUNTY REGIONAL HISTORY CENTER.

that was as its center. He built a large tourist hotel called Tonyawaha (Ton-ya-wa-ha), meaning healing waters. The new name did not take hold, and the area continued to be called Clay Springs.

CURRYVILLE

Curryville was an African American community located east of Chuluota at the end of old Fort Christmas Road. In the 1910s and 1920s, Curryville operated as a turpentine camp, and families lived in shacks scattered in the camp area. Men were paid the equivalent of ten cents per hour in script which could only be used at the camp commissary.

After D. W. Curry discontinued his turpentine business, sawmill operators moved to Curryville and employed African Americans, who adapted to changing work environments out of necessity. As in many communities dependent upon one industry, Curryville could not sustain residents after the sawmills closed.

FOREST CITY

There were a few grove owners already in the area when Forest City was platted in 1883. Its heart was where state roads 436 and 434 intersect today, and it had a schoolhouse, railroad depot, general store, and boarding-house. After the big freezes in 1894 and 1895, Frank Pounds started a sawmill, producing wooden crates for shipping fruit.

By the 1950s, the plant had 2,000 employees in 20 buildings for packing, storing, and processing concentrate. With the plant's expansion and the sprawl of suburbia, the town gradually faded away. The plant changed hands several times, and finally Coca-Cola bought the operation for its Minute Maid product line. The landmark citrus plant closed after the 1983 freeze, and the crossroads that defined Forest City became part of a sprawling business complex connecting Apopka and Altamonte Springs.

GAINSBORO

George T. Gaines and his two sons founded Gainsboro in 1886 with the intent of making it a railroad station serving Tangerine. It was located about two miles west of Zellwood on the south side of Lake Ola and had a wide street that ran around the lake to Tangerine.

Gaines had a nursery where he sold sour root stock. The town had a general store and a Presbyterian church. Its sawmill did a brisk business in building lumber as well as orange boxes and vegetable crates. There were several citrus groves and a turpentine still with turpentine camps nearby. By the 1920s, Gainsboro also vanished because of the downturn in the local economy.

GRASMERE

Grasmere, a town less than one mile from Zellwood, had its own post office and train

station by 1885, but its legacy today is school busing. As the result of the consolidation of small schools in 1920, Grasmere and Plymouth students were the first to be "bused" at public expense. They traveled by a horse-drawn wagon to school in Apopka. As transportation in Florida improved, the need for so many separate communities within short distances diminished. Plymouth survived; Grasmere did not.

JONESTOWN

Jonestown was Orlando's first African American community. Prominent businessman James Magruder built the settlement in the late 1800s and named it after Jonestown's first settlers, Sam and Penney Jones. Located on the east side of Orlando, Jonestown was an area roughly bounded by Brown and Bumby Avenues and East Jackson and Anderson Streets. The community's homes had two or three bedrooms with porches and tin roofs. Most people had vegetable gardens and a yard for chickens. Some had room for hogs and a cow.

Disaster hit Jonestown in 1904 when nearby Fern Creek swelled and a sink hole overflowed, causing major flooding. Floodwaters rose nearly to the roofs of some of the one-story homes. Following another flood, city officials declared Jonestown a slum and had it demolished in 1941. Homeowners received small sums of money, but most could not afford to buy homes elsewhere.

Before Jonestown's demolition, white Orlando residents had been complaining about blacks living on the east side of the railroad tracks. Consequently, they were moved to Griffin Park, a public housing project in the existing black community on the west side of town. The Jonestown area now is Reeves Terrace and probably part of the East-West Expressway.

LAKEVILLE

Founded in 1884, Lakeville was about three miles south of Apopka and two miles southwest of Piedmont. Many local residents shared interest in the town's development. C. O. Warner's real estate office advertised pine land from twenty to forty dollars per acre. In the late 1880s, the Warner House became the town's tourist hotel, and Warner also had cottages for rent on Lake Apopka. Local grove owner N. M. Cogswell was an important pioneer in the development of the state's citrus industry.

MARKHAM

William Markham purchased land in 1875 and founded the Markham settlement near Wekiwa Springs. African Americans

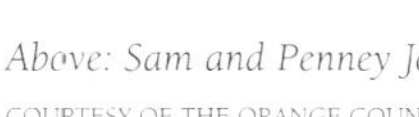

Above: Sam and Penney Jones.

COURTESY OF THE ORANGE COUNTY REGIONAL HISTORY CENTER.

Below: Jonestown was prone to flooding.

COURTESY OF THE ORANGE COUNTY REGIONAL HISTORY CENTER.

developed the lumber, turpentine, and agricultural commerce there in the early 1880s. By the end of the decade, the community had a post office, and the Sanford and Lake Eustis Railway served the area. After the turn of the century, the Overstreet Turpentine Company acquired land in the area. Today, the land is vacant where the church and cemetery once stood, and it is part of the state park system.

MCDONALD

McDonald was a community built around a railroad station about a mile from Plymouth. It served the Merrimack community about two miles away. Its first setter, Andrew A. McDonald arrived in 1873 from Virginia with his daughter and five sons. The eldest son was a doctor and practiced medicine in McDonald and Zellwood during the 1880s. Although all of the sons were interested in the grove business, only Marian Fitzhugh remained after the freezes of the mid-1890s. He became a major citrus grower and was a charter member of the Plymouth Citrus Growers Association until his death in 1936.

MERRIMACK

Merrimack was founded between present-day Errol Estates and Poncan Road in 1875 by settlers from Manchester, New Hampshire. They named the town after the Merrimack River in New Hampshire. The town grew and by 1882, settlers of neighboring communities admired the local school that had been built for $500. By 1925, Merrimack ceased to exist.

PIEDMONT

Swedish settlers Olaf and Johanna Larson founded Piedmont on Christmas Eve in 1877. They planted citrus on their homestead, and soon other Swedes migrated to the area. Piedmont prospered and, by the mid-1880s, the town had a schoolhouse and general store. Two railroads served the town's transportation needs.

Largely dependent on the citrus industry, central Florida suffered from devastating freezes in 1894-95. Many people left because they did not have the money to wait for new grove production. However, most Piedmont settlers stayed and relied on one another to get through hard times.

They removed the dead trunks and planted vegetable gardens. They fenced in land and raised cattle. Barnyard animals like ducks, geese, and chicken also helped sustain them. When cattle or hogs were slaughtered, neighbors shared the bounty.

By 1905, Piedmont had a post office and was a growing community. Locals shipped lumber and produce to northern markets on the Atlantic Coast Line. Citrus was on its way back but, by 1908, the railroad was gone, and Piedmont had to rely on other stations for shipment.

Due to a variety of reasons, Apopka became the center for commerce for northwest Orange County. The train no longer came, most students attended Apopka schools, and Piedmont's post office moved to Apopka in 1922. By 1941, Piedmont no longer existed on most local maps. Today the area is recognizable primarily by Piedmont-Wekiwa Road.

ORANGE CENTER/ VINELAND

Vineland was a town bordering Lake Ruby near the southern end of what today is Apopka-Vineland Road, but it was originally called Orange Center until the name changed in 1918. It started as a real estate sales gimmick when the Munger Land Company developed 5-acre lots from its vast land holdings. Between 1910 and 1912, the company gave away a 25-by-120-foot lot with each five-acre purchase. By 1911, Orange Center was recorded in the Orange County plat book, and on January 31, 1912, the post office opened.

On July 20, 1918, the post office name changed to Vineland after three brothers planted a small vineyard as another real estate promotion. Additional settlers also attempted to grow grapes, but a grape disease wiped out all of the vineyards. During the 1920s, the town center had stores, the post office, a school, a railroad depot, and a peak population of 120 residents. When the Atlantic Coast Line spur was abandoned, the town began to decline and, in 1940, the post office closed.

Vineland was the last town in Orange County to get electricity, but it was the first to get Disney. The once quiet little community bordered the twenty-seven-thousand-acre tract that Walt Disney originally purchased. Today, there are still interconnecting roads that lead to nowhere, remnants of early platting, and the area has become a Muslim community containing a mosque and school.

CONCLUSION

Now, travelers drive State Road 17-92 from Orlando to Winter Park in minutes. One hundred years ago, these two cities were separated by Wilcox and Formosa, and it took hours to travel from one to the other. Without a sign, it is difficult for the untrained eye to know where many of the remaining small towns begin and end as sprawl throughout Orange County unites the area into a metropolis.

Opposite, top: The 1890 Piedmont School.

COURTESY OF THE ORANGE COUNTY REGIONAL HISTORY CENTER

Opposite, middle: Vineland got its name from the many vineyards in the area.

COURTESY OF THE ORANGE COUNTY REGIONAL HISTORY CENTER

Opposite, bottom: Residents of Piedmont gather for a group photograph, c. 1870.

COURTESY OF THE ORANGE COUNTY REGIONAL HISTORY CENTER

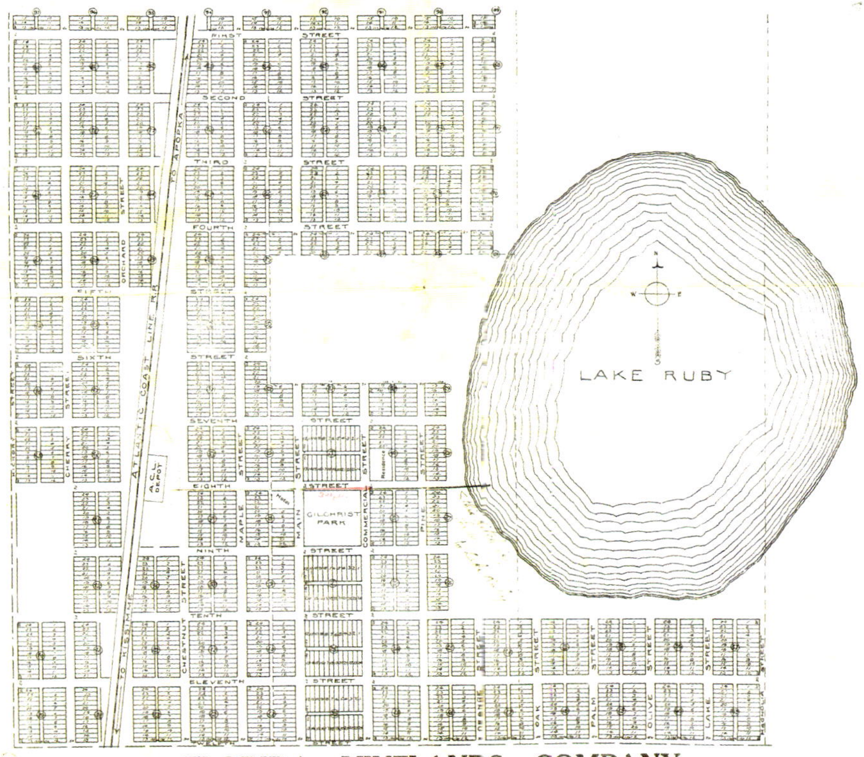

Below: A portion of the land shown on this map is now part of the land owned by Walt Disney World.

COURTESY OF THE ORANGE COUNTY REGIONAL HISTORY CENTER

Lake Eola Band Shell, c. 1925.
COURTESY OF THE ORANGE COUNTY REGIONAL HISTORY CENTER.

SHARING THE HERITAGE

Historic profiles of businesses, organizations, and families that have contributed to the development and economic base of Orange County

Special Thanks to

Brant & Son, Inc.

Springhill Suites by Marriott

Florida Hospital

Florida Hospital is owned and operated by Adventist Health System, a part of the worldwide organization of Seventh-day Adventist Church. Although the hospital has experienced revolutionary change over the past century, it remains a Christ-centered organization with a purpose that is well stated in its Mission Statement: "Our first responsibility as a Christian hospital is to extend the healing ministry of Christ to all patients who come to us."

Above: The two-story farmhouse that became the first Florida Hospital building in 1908.

Right: The Medical Director's exam room in the early twentieth century.

Today's billion-dollar Florida Hospital system was started with only $4.83 and a lot of faith. Four dollars and eighty-three cents was all the cash Seventh-day Adventist leaders had in their treasury, when they made an offer to purchase what was then known as the "Dr. Harris Sanitorium and Hotel Company." But church members had an unlimited amount of faith.

The facility had been established by Orlando surgeon R.L. Harris in a farmhouse located on seventy-two acres between the shores of Lake Estelle and Lake Winyah. At the time, the facility was a tuberculosis sanatorium and the confusion between "TB sanitorium" and a "hospital sanitarium" would linger for decades until the hospital dropped the word from its name in 1970.

Dr. Harris built several small cottages on the property, installed a sewer system, and outfitted the rooms, spending a total of $12,500, considered a large sum in those days.

The TB facility, however, failed to prosper and Dr. Harris moved to Jacksonville to practice surgery, leaving the future of the sanitorium in serious jeopardy. In the spring of 1908, the property came to the attention of the leaders of the Florida Conference of Seventh-day Adventists, who felt it would be a wonderful location for a health facility they had been hoping to establish in Central Florida.

The church leaders, however, had a serious problem. The funds on hand totaled only $4.83. After much prayer and counsel, they decided to make an offer of $9,000 and rely on God's goodness to provide the funds. The offer was refused at first, but finally accepted. By the time the offer was accepted, the Conference had managed to raise the needed funds, with one church member even selling his home to make the purchase possible.

The farmhouse originally purchased by Dr. Harris continued to be the facility's main building for several years. The two-story structure with wraparound porches could handle twenty patients and included surgery facilities, rehabilitation program, and a maternity unit. Amenities reflected the taste and wealth of many of the patients, including an ornate parlor, elegant dining room and a spacious lobby, which resembled a hotel lobby.

A number of major improvements occurred from 1908 until 1920, setting a pattern of expansion that continues today. A new two-and-a-half story wing, one of the first in the area to be constructed of concrete block,

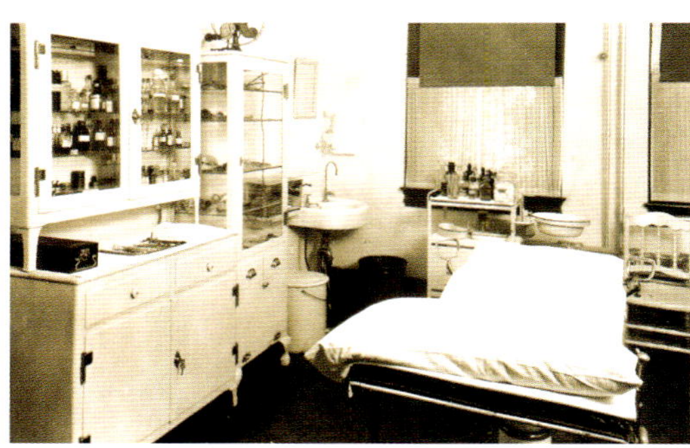

was added in 1912, raising the hospital's capacity to sixty beds. In 1918 the building was enlarged to three stories and doubled in length, bringing capacity to 100 beds. A medical unit was also added at this time. A South Wing was constructed in 1925, connecting the 1908 and 1912 buildings.

During the 1920s and 1930s, the hospital catered to the true "sanitarium patient,"

including many patients who came from the North and spent the entire winter in the hospital facility. Many were not really "ill" in today's sense of the word, but came seeking the warm climate along with rest and relaxation. These patients expected to be entertained and treated in an atmosphere of refined elegance.

The slower pace of sanitarium-style care continued through this era, but physicians were beginning to place more emphasis on the hospital's medical and surgical programs. Assuming the role of family practitioners, these physicians practiced medicine, performed surgery, delivered babies, and did most anything else that was required.

A one-story wing to house treatment rooms was added in 1938 and, in 1940, a West Wing opened, adding eighteen surgical beds, operating rooms, delivery rooms and a doctor's lounge. A North Wing constructed in 1949 nearly doubled bed capacity, bringing it to 160 beds.

In 1958 the administrator at the time–Leighton Hall–made an improvement that would change the way the hospital operated forever; he installed air conditioning. Florida Sanitarium became the first air conditioned hospital in Central Florida, allowing the facility to operate year-round for the first time, a novelty greatly appreciated by physicians, staff, patients and visitors alike.

When Don Welch became administrator in 1961, the hospital had only a few board-certified physicians and there was a great need to improve the medical staff. Within just a few weeks, Welch and a new medical staff director, Jack Allen, MD re-wrote the medical staff by-laws to require certification for surgeons and strengthening the disciplinary process for any physicians providing substandard care. They also strengthened the credentialing process to ensure that new additions to the staff would be well-trained.

"Improving the medical staff was the key to every good thing that happened," says Welch. "Word got around pretty quickly that things were changing for the better. That's when we started seeing more patients come to the hospital and the growth has never really stopped since that time. It's pretty amazing when you look back and see how far the hospital has come."

In 1970 the hospital changed its name, dropping the word "sanitarium" which seemed inappropriate for the modern era.

In 1971 the facility became the first hospital in the nation to install the Howarth-Charnley Clean Air Suite (laminar air flow room), a new approach that would revolutionize joint replacement surgery. By using air filtering to control the level of environmental pollutants such as dust, airborne microbes, aerosol particles and chemical vapors, the suite greatly reduces the chances of infection to the patient.

The early 1970s also saw development of another new specialty, organ retrieval and transplantation. The first kidney transplant was performed in 1973 and, today, the hospital is a regional transplant center ranking among the busiest in the nation. The hospital underwent another temporary name change in the 1980s when it was called Florida Hospital Medical Center.

In 2007, Walt Disney World and Disney Worldwide Outreach announced a $10 million contribution to Disney Children's Hospital at Florida Hospital, a 155-bed, full-service facility served by sixty Kid's Docs, the largest panel of pediatric specialists in Orlando, and a highly trained pediatric team of more than 600 employees.

The decades that followed included a number of 'firsts' for Florida Hospital,

Above: A view of Florida Hospital from across Lake Estelle. Circa 1970s.

Below: Florida Hospital's focus and dedication to pediatric care is second to none.

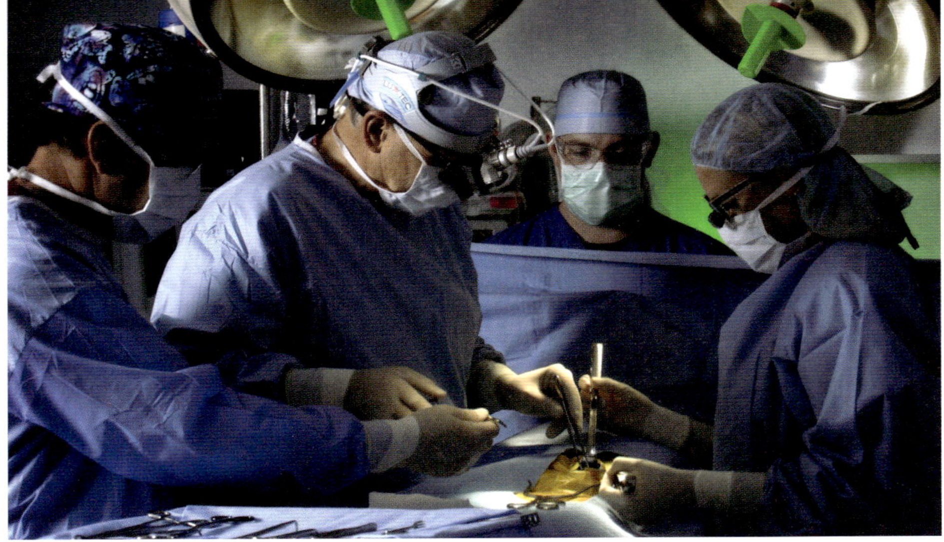

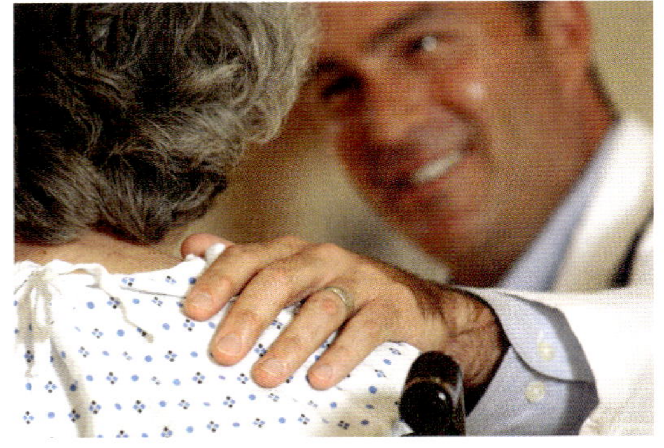

Top, left: Florida Hospital provides care from superior physicians with the latest in medical technology.

Top, right: At Florida Hospital a helping hand is never far away.

including installation of one of the nation's first CT scanners, the first angioplasty, the first hospital in central Florida to install an MRI, the first in Florida to have the GE Light Speed CT Scanner that allows for six times faster scanning of images, and the first in the state to offer clinical digital mammography.

Today, the Florida Hospital name is found on seven hospitals in Central Florida, as well as on dozens of other businesses which provide outpatient services, medical equipment and other medical goods and services. The main campus of Florida Hospital is located at 601 East Rollins Street in Orlando, with other facilities located in Altamonte, Apopka, East Orlando, Kissimmee, Winter Park and Celebration. The hospital is part of the comprehensive network of seventeen hospitals of the Adventist Health System–Florida Division.

Since the turn of the twenty-first century, Florida Hospital has pioneered such medical advancements as implanted digital pacemakers, the first inpatient facility in Central Florida for pediatric seizure monitoring, and DaVinci™ robotic-assisted surgery for radical prostatectomy. The hospital was also the first in Central Florida to offer PET/CT technology, 4D ultrasound and mini-hip replacement.

From its modest beginnings a century ago, Florida Hospital has grown into an acute-care health care system with 2,204 beds throughout Central Florida. Florida Hospital treats more than one million patient visits each year, making it the largest system in the country for treating patients. Florida Hospital offers a wide range of health services for the entire family, including many nationally and internationally recognized programs in cardiology, cancer, diabetes, digestive health, pediatrics, women's medicine, neurology/neurosurgery and orthopaedics. The hospital is the only Central Florida facility to earn national recognition from *U.S. News & World Report* as "One of America's Best Hospitals" for diabetes care and has been on the list for ten years.

Florida Hospital has earned a national reputation as a leader in advanced cardiac care and has become known as "America's Heart Hospital." Because Florida Hospital performs more complex cardiac cases than any other facility in the country, MSNBC selected the hospital as the premier focus of an hour-long special, *America's Heart Hospital*. Each year, our team of 130 board-certified cardiologists and cardiovascular surgeons, and more than a thousand specially trained cardiac nurses and technicians, treat more heart patients than any other hospital in the nation.

As the first of its kind in Central Florida, the Nicholson Center for Surgical Advancement is a premier center for hands-on surgical instruction. The prime objective is to develop and disseminate cutting edge surgical knowledge and techniques to the global surgical community through state-of-the-art teleconferencing technology. Participants perform minimally invasive surgical procedures at one of nine state-of-the-art endoscopically equipped stations.

Recent additions at Florida Hospital include a new five-story, 200,000 square foot addition at Florida Hospital East Orlando. This tower adds eighty private rooms and allows for more outpatient services.

A new six-story patient tower at Florida Hospital Altamonte will increase access to health care for Seminole county residents. The $70 million tower adds seventy-two patient beds in addition to a new chapel and healing garden.

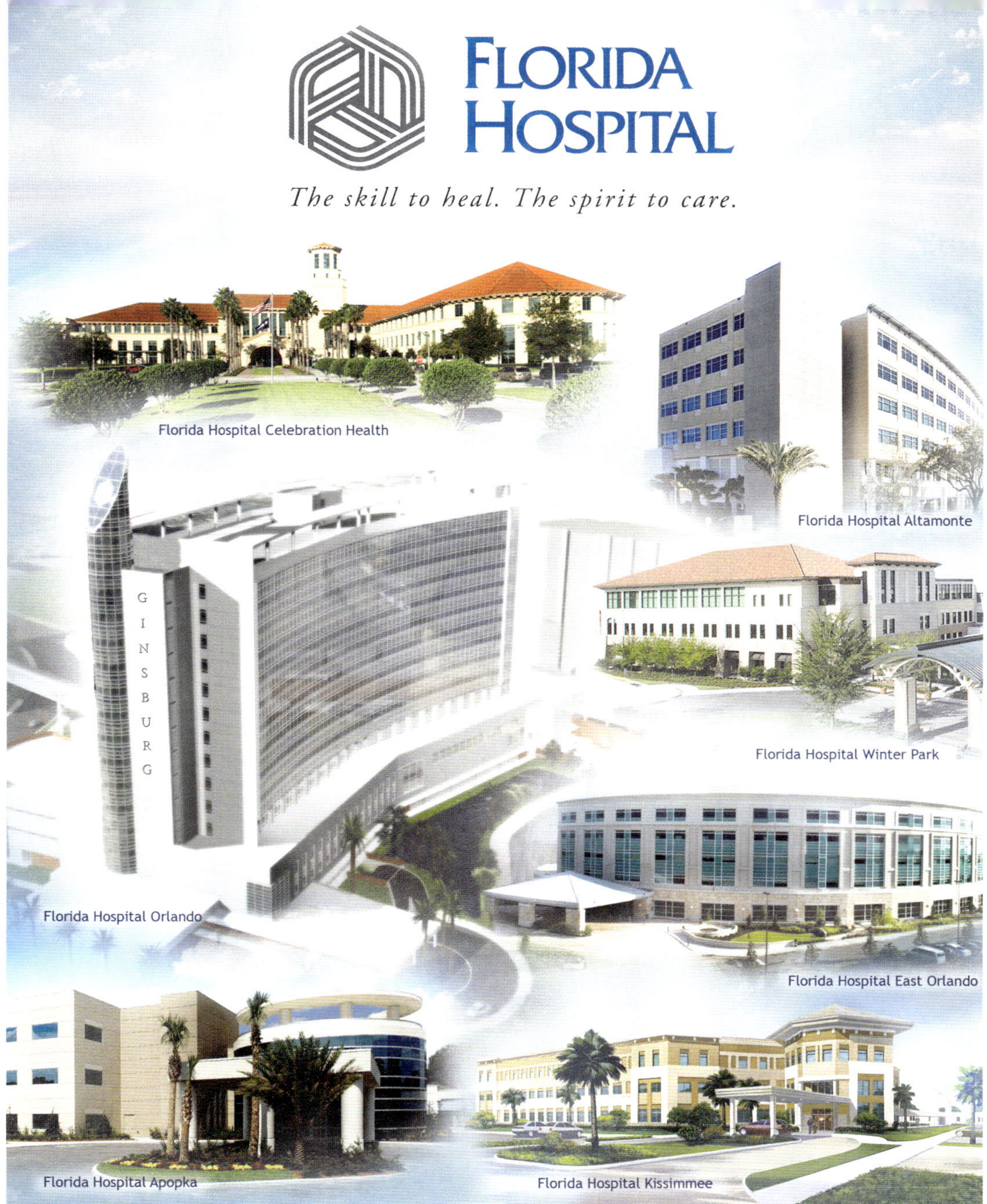

Florida Hospital Orlando recently opened a 15-story, 660,000 square foot addition with 440 new patient rooms. The addition houses the Florida Hospital Cardiovascular Institute which includes fourteen cardiac catheterization labs, and one of the largest Emergency Departments in the nation with sixty-three examination rooms. The commitment from Disney laid the foundation for the "Children's Hospital of the Future." By 2010 the seven-story, $40 million Disney Children's Hospital at Florida Hospital will have a total of 200 dedicated pediatric beds; a dedicated pediatric Emergency Department, and an Advanced Center for Pediatric Surgery.

While current hospital President Lars Houmann and his administrative staff have sought ways to contain costs for patients while maintaining the high standards that support "the skill to heal," the "spirit to care" has also been of primary importance.

The Volunteer Visitors in Pastoral Care program, which began in the early 1990s, has trained more than a hundred volunteers whose work with the hospital's patients and their families has greatly enhanced the hospital's mission of caring for the "whole person: physical, emotional and spiritual." The hospital's community outreach programs have also grown and expanded over the years. Then, as now, these programs have included education about healthy lifestyles, good nutrition, exercise, fresh air, emotional health, spiritual growth and a positive outlook on life.

For more information about Florida Hospital, check the website at www.floridahospital.com.

Kelsey Construction, Inc.

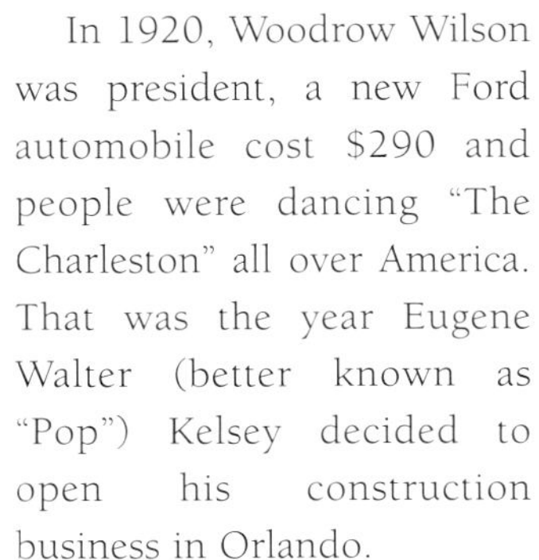

In 1920, Woodrow Wilson was president, a new Ford automobile cost $290 and people were dancing "The Charleston" all over America. That was the year Eugene Walter (better known as "Pop") Kelsey decided to open his construction business in Orlando.

In those days construction was regarded as more of a trade than an industry, but Pop had a vision that his local construction company could sustain his whole family... and he was right. Today, Kelsey Construction, Inc.'s newest vice president is Courtney Kelsey Peacock, a fourth generation Kelsey who is following in the footsteps of her great-grandfather.

Courtney teamed up with her dad, Mike, who serves as president, in 2002. A Rollins MBA grad, Courtney also received her LEED (Leadership in Energy and Environmental Design) accreditation. It is the nationally accepted benchmark for the design, construction and operation of high-performance green buildings. Great-granddad would have been so proud! Perhaps he knew when women first voted in a national election back in 1920 that one day his great-granddaughter would be stepping into a leadership role in the family business! And Courtney was certainly honoring her family roots when she obtained her Florida General Contractor's License. Pop's son, Gene (Courtney's grandfather, Mike's dad) wrote the first contractors' license exam in Orange County and was widely regarded as the "go to" guy for other general contractors who wanted a bit of coaching on how to prepare for the exam.

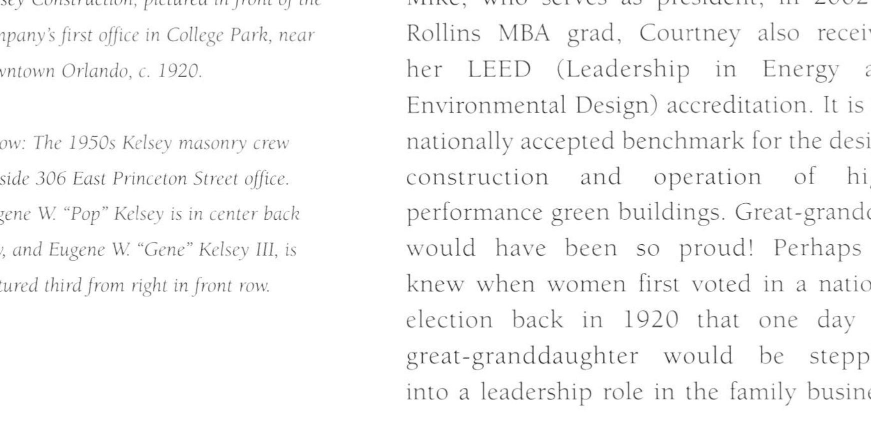

Above: Eugene W. "Pop" Kelsey, founder of Kelsey Construction, pictured in front of the company's first office in College Park, near downtown Orlando, c. 1920.

Below: The 1950s Kelsey masonry crew outside 306 East Princeton Street office. Eugene W. "Pop" Kelsey is in center back row, and Eugene W. "Gene" Kelsey III, is pictured third from right in front row.

Mike grew up working summers on construction projects and learning the trade. "My grandfather used to take me to his jobsites and show me his work when I was just a little guy," the Furman University grad says proudly. The family business that started out building homes for residents of Orlando's growing community in 1920 has kept its focus on great-granddad's personal mission: "Honesty and honoring the Lord in every decision, and quality workmanship is always a goal." The company has been blessed with wonderful employees and great clients over the years; and that attitude could be the reason most Kelsey employees are long-timers, even now. More than two-thirds of Kelsey's employees have been on the payroll for more than ten years. As the oldest homegrown general contractor in Central Florida, the Kelsey

Construction philosophy is a testament to the real benefit of having quality people perform quality workmanship.

Residential construction was the staple of the family business in the early years, but it was not long before Orlando's business climate became sophisticated and needed nice new buildings. The Orlando skyline of today bears little resemblance to its image of the '20s, but there are some examples of early Kelsey fingerprints in the downtown core to this day. Many Kelsey-built churches, schools and downtown office buildings in Orlando's central business district are still in use and literally stand as beacons of another Kelsey motto: "Built to last."

In the '30s, the Kelsey headquarters was in Orlando's College Park district. From this central location, the Kelsey team began to branch out in all directions throughout Central Florida, tackling the notion of building the very popular, "newfangled" (as Pop would say) retail centers. The idea of people parking their cars in one spot and then shopping conveniently in several stores in the fresh Florida sunshine was catching on quickly in Central Florida, and Kelsey Construction was ready to make it happen!

The rest, as they say, is history. It was not long before the retail centers led to warehouse and distribution facilities, office buildings and high-rise parking garages. Once Kelsey got a taste of the large-scale construction projects, there was no holding back. The Kelsey team was sought out for the biggest and the best. Orange County's most secure correctional facilities are Kelsey products, as are Central Florida military installations and even themed entertainment venues. And, although many of Kelsey's completed projects over eight decades have earned industry awards and various community distinctions, perhaps the centerpiece of Kelsey's impressive list of accomplishments is the Orange County Convention Center. At nearly two million square feet of exhibit space, it ranks as one of the finest convention and trade show facilities in the world.

Above: First Presbyterian Church on Church Street, built by Kelsey in the1960s and expanded several times since, remains an active area of worship in downtown Orlando.

Below: A dramatic evening view of the world-renowned Orange County Convention Center. Kelsey constructed Phases III and IV in the early '90s and received national recognition for Orange County.

Former Orange County Chairman Linda W. Chapin still beams when she talks about the significance of her last public construction project. "The Kelsey team worked at a frenzied pace, in an occupied facility that never closes, for many months to meet our deadlines," she says. "As a result, our Convention Center is a magnificent tourism banner for Orange County to wave, of course," she noted. "At the same time, it is also widely recognized as one of the most highly successful public facilities in the state."

And, while the building itself has received numerous accolades; one honor is a special source of pride for the whole Kelsey organization. The National Association of Counties selected Minority/Women Business Enterprise Construction Management Program for its 1995 Achievement Award. Under Mike's guidance and leadership, the Kelsey team at the Convention Center was responsible for the successful development and implementation of the largest M/WBE program ever established in the state of Florida.

"When we were selected to receive the award from the National Association of Counties for our general contractor's construction management program," said Convention Center CEO Tom Ackert, "I couldn't wait to call Mike Kelsey to share that news. It was an historic moment for Orange County, and we have the Kelsey team to thank for it."

There are historic moments projected for the future, as well. The Tradition Towers project is slated to be the tallest building in downtown Orlando. Tradition Towers is comprised of twin towers connected by a glass-enclosed bridge that overlooks the west shore of Lake Eola, and will house the city's prestigious University Club, office condominiums and residential suites. As a member of the Tradition Tower's team, Kelsey Construction looks forward to the continuation of its role in making downtown history.

In 1920, one guy could be hired to do nearly every aspect of getting a job built. He might have been the designer, the builder, the painter and the electrician. He might have poured the concrete and also planted the shrubs. That was Pop Kelsey. Today's Kelsey team is really no different. There are staff professionals from all areas of the construction field; and they employ the same resourcefulness and guarantee the same reliability great-granddad was so famous for.

In addition to that most reliable of antique construction tools, the transit, today's Kelsey

Above: A rendering of Tradition Towers, designed to be Orlando's tallest new building and scheduled to be Kelsey-built across the street from the Public Library at the intersection of Magnolia Avenue and Central Boulevard, overlooking the eastern shore of Lake Eola.

Below: Millenia Lakes Office Building, a 206,000 square feet example of Kelsey-built "Class A" office space with twenty-six acres of site improvements and an extension of Millenia Lakes Boulevard, c. 2001.

team puts technology to its highest and best use. Perhaps one of the most popular services Kelsey offers its clients is real-time Webcam feedback so that they can monitor construction progress at any time. If Pop thought all the post-war shopping centers were "newfangled," what do you suppose he would say about Webcams and his great grand-daughter's Blackberry? Well, one thing we know for sure, he was always happy to show his clients the progress on their jobs; and if they could have watched that success on a computer screen, so much the better!

Lest anyone get the impression that the Kelsey legacy has been completely laid out and measured by the city's tallest buildings and miles of air-conditioned spaces, there is a soft, quiet side to the family business, too. Mike's dad, Gene, knew the value of community service and signed the company up for a founding membership in the Central Florida Builders' Exchange (CFBE) back in the early '40s and was also a charter member of the fledgling national association of general contractors, later to be named the Association of General Contractors (AGC).

Mike currently serves as the chair of the Central Florida SunTrust Advisory Board, an organization whose founders' slogan of "Build Your community and You Build Your Bank" mirrors Mike's own personal view of things. Like his dad and his grandfather before him, his volunteer commitments nearly equal his hours in the field. Having served on committees for the CFBE, Mike also has lent his construction expertise to the City of Orlando's Municipal Planning Board and the Builders' Exchange Federal Credit Union. As chair of the building Committee for the First Baptist Church, Mike supervised the historic move from its downtown location to the present First Baptist headquarters facility south of town. The heartfelt words of a former Kelsey client, T. Andrew Pughe, who worked with the Kelsey team on the construction of the Arthur J. Williams Chapel at the Edgewood Children's Ranch, express the views of many who have enjoyed a Kelsey construction experience: "It is a much better facility than we ever imagined, and we know it was a labor of love for you and your staff."

Yes, since 1920, that is the way the Kelsey Construction Company works. For additional information on Kelsey Construction Company, visit www.kelseyconstruction.com.

Above: Eugene Kelsey, Courtney Kelsey Peacock, and Mike Kelsey stop working long enough to pose for a photo in front of a Kelsey site sign, c. 2008.

Below: Publix, c. 2006. Kelsey's role included demolition of the old grocery store and construction of the new twenty-seven-thousand-square-foot Publix, built to reflect old architecture and preserve the façade under a "fast-track" completion schedule to accommodate the area's residents.

Crittenden Fruit Company, Inc.

The founder and president of Crittenden Fruit Company, Earl M. Crittenden—known to all as "Duke"—was born and raised in Orlando. He has been an Indian River citrus grower since the 1950s and organized Crittenden Fruit Company in 1959.

Duke, who likes to say, "Nobody ever went broke taking a profit," currently owns thousands of acres of orange, grapefruit, and tangerine groves across Florida and operates one of the state's largest fresh fruit packing operations.

Crittenden Fruit Company's mission statement is: "To run a successful, honest, full-service citrus company," and to this end the company plants all its own trees.

Before organizing Crittenden Fruit Company, Duke and Shine Hardman operated Acme Fruit Company for five years. It was during that period that Duke learned firsthand the uncertainties of the citrus business.

In December 1957, Florida experienced its first significant freeze since the early 1930s and '40s. A way was needed to salvage the thousands of acres of citrus by converting it to orange concentrate, which meant finding a place that could pasteurize with heat and store one-half million boxes.

Duke and Shine met with Bill, Rudus, and Bud Cook of B. C. Cook and Sons, which had the largest operation in the citrus business at the time—even million boxes per year.

Henry Nehrling stands amongst Alocasia Odora, a large elephant ear plant that is native to Southeast Asia. Florida is the only place in the United States where this plant can be found today.

COURTESY OF THE ORANGE COUNTY REGIONAL HISTORY CENTER

The Lake Highland facility had closed down, but the Cook brothers contacted them and learned the plant could be up and running in three to four days. Acme took over the facility and ran 20,000 boxes of citrus per day, 10,000 for the Cooks, and 10,000 for Acme. The fruit from the bad freeze was held until October and the operators were able to net $5-$6 on the tree cost, which equals eighty cents delivered to the processing plant.

In the summer of 1972, Duke decided to move from Maitland and relocate to Groveland and build a new packinghouse, which shipped more than three million cartons each year.

In recent years, Crittenden has expanded its real estate holdings, which are now the largest part of the business. "Orange groves are a big tax shelter," Duke notes. "We planted groves on the best land in Central Florida and the land could be sold for housing without recapturing the depreciation."

Duke Crittenden is a former member of the Florida Citrus Commission and former chairman of the Growers Administrative Committee. Crittenden is a supporter of Lake Highland Preparatory School and Orlando Remembered, and is a long-time member of Florida Citrus Mutual.

The Albin Polasek Museum & Sculpture Gardens honors the career of internationally renowned sculptor Albin Polasek. The Czech-born artist retired in Winter Park.

COURTESY OF THE ORANGE COUNTY REGIONAL HISTORY CENTER

FISHER, RUSHMER, WERRENRATH, DICKSON, TALLEY & DUNLAP, P.A.

The law firm of Fisher, Rushmer, Werrenrath, Dickson, Talley & Dunlap, P.A. has invested in the Central Florida community for more than a quarter of a century. Fisher Rushmer represents clients throughout the state, region, and beyond, in sectors including construction, transportation, real estate, insurance, tourism and hospitality, engineering and design, employment, entertainment and healthcare.

From families and smaller "mom and pop" businesses, to mid-sized, commercial and Fortune 500 companies, Fisher Rushmer has served a variety of clients for over twenty-five years. The firm is positioned to continue that legacy as our community and state grows.

Located in the heart of downtown Orlando at Orange Avenue and Central Boulevard, Fisher Rushmer started in 1984 with only eleven attorneys and has since tripled its size. The firm has earned the highest possible rating from Martindale-Hubbell, the country's pre-eminent legal rating service. All of the firm's senior attorneys are also individually ranked with the highest possible rating, and several are Board Certified in Civil Trial Law by The Florida Bar. Over the years, the firm's attorneys have held positions of leadership in The Florida Bar—including on the board of governors—and have served on committees and boards of the Orange County Bar Association.

Above: Shareholder (from left) James Talley and Frank Rapprich visit a construction site in downtown Orlando.

Below: Shareholder Keersten Heskin Martinez and Associate Christopher Harne represent family law clients, and serve as guardians ad litem for children. Emma Lewis is pictured with her grandmother, Beverly Frible.

Fisher Rushmer has always been committed to delivering quality legal services. The firm is especially known for its civil trial experience, and holds a statewide reputation for its appellate practice.

The reason Fisher Rushmer lawyers are effective is simple: its attorneys are passionate about the law and are committed to delivering exceptional legal services. Fisher Rushmer attorneys care about every client and every case. "We have the reputation for going the extra mile—for being prepared and accepting any challenge," says founding shareholder John Fisher.

Upon the firm's formation, the founding lawyers practiced primarily in the area of insurance litigation. However, since then, Fisher Rushmer has significantly expanded its focus to include a wide range of practice areas, representing clients from either the plaintiff or the defense perspective. All of the firm's attorneys are ready to face twenty-first century legal challenges, from catastrophic personal injury and wrongful death matters to complex commercial litigation, real estate transactions, or business and shareholder/partner disputes.

Extensive litigation, courtroom and appellate experience have made the firm a top choice for many clients seeking litigation counsel. With its commercial and corporate background, the firm represents organizations

in contract matters, stock and investment fraud cases, and unfair competition and trade practice cases. Other firm practices include employment and discrimination law, professional liability suits, and insurance and bad faith cases. The firm recently established a mediation and dispute resolution group that assists clients looking to avoid litigation and lengthy legal battles. Fisher Rushmer's health law experience attracts physicians, large practitioner groups and other healthcare organizations. The firm's appellate practice has handled major tort and negligence decisions throughout Florida and across the country. A team of in-house consultants, including nurses and paralegals, provide technical assistance with all matters.

Fisher Rushmer's dedication to clients carries over to a commitment to the community. The firm's attorneys make it a priority to give back to Central Florida by contributing time and energy to several charitable groups including Meals on Wheels, The Mustard Seed, House of Hope and the Central Florida Chapter of the American Red Cross. Many of the firm's lawyers also hold leadership positions in these groups.

Since its establishment, Fisher Rushmer has been recognized for its pro bono service to the needy and indigent. Through the Legal Aid Society of the Orange County Bar Association, Fisher Rushmer attorneys have logged tens of thousands of hours of free legal work to low-income residents, the working poor and the area's disadvantaged.

Fisher Rushmer cares particularly about the children of Central Florida, and its attorneys often serve as guardians *ad litem* in cases involving allegations of abuse, abandonment or neglect.

Through the years, the firm has been awarded many honors for its pro bono service. In 2008, Fisher Rushmer was chosen as a "Law Firm of Excellence" for its tireless contributions to the Legal Aid Society.

Everyone at Fisher Rushmer is dedicated to delivering excellence, and that commitment has built a statewide and regional reputation that is second to none. "Each of us brings exceptional attributes to the mix, all the while understanding the meaning and importance of teamwork," says Fisher. "I am proud of what we have accomplished these past twenty-five years, and look forward to seeing what the future holds for us."

Fisher, Rushmer, Werrenrath, Dickson, Talley & Dunlap, P.A. is located at 20 North Orange Avenue in downtown Orlando. For additional information about the firm, please visit www.fisherlawfirm.com.

Above: Fisher Rushmer shareholders include (sitting from left) James Talley, Gary Rushmer, John Fisher, Reinald Werrenrath, Karel Averill, (standing from left) Lora Dunlap, Keersten Heskin Martinez, Chris Bellentine, David Corso, Russell Dickson, Philip King, Jon Oden and Richard Smith. Not pictured: Joseph Amos, Jonathan Hollingshead, Jeffrey Kirsheman, Jamie Billotte Moses, Stephanie Preston, Frank Rapprich and Emery Rosenbluth.

Below: Shareholders (from left) David Corso, Joseph Amos, Jonathan Hollingshead and Karel Averill litigate cases for local, statewide and national clients.

Florida Crown Development Corp. & Subsidiaries

Webb International, Inc.

William C Webb Company

"It's 1986 and we are busy planning a new 1,700 acre business park located just west of the Orlando airport called the Airport Industrial Park at Orlando. Sand Lake Road and Orange Avenue are two lane roads. Tradeport Drive terminates at the airport Post Office and we are working with the City and Airport Authority to make its connection into Orange Avenue. We are on the outskirts of town, the new kid on the block, and we need a customer to put the park on the map. The telephone rings, it's Bud Whittaker (alias 007) with CSX business development and he has just the customer we need; GE. They need CSX rail, and good access to the transportation network. We have neither, but we have great plans for both and a belief that we can get the job done. So how to convince GE when we don't even have a road to the site? We start clearing, earthmoving, and hire a helicopter to show the site. We said we are sure this is where your new 350,000 square foot distribution center will be located, so we have started construction. Shortly afterward we receive the call that they accept our proposal. Eight months after signing the lease, GE took occupancy of the building, the park was on the map."

This story began when William C. "Bill" Webb launched his construction career shortly after World War II, as a carpenter for a general contractor. A fifth generation Floridian, Webb was educated at the University of Miami but learned his business from the ground up, as carpenter, foreman, construction superintendent, and entrepreneur.

The William C. Webb family has been a positive force in building Florida's future for more than half-a-century through innovation and an uncompromising commitment to quality. Founder Bill Webb earned international recognition as the developer of the first master-planned industrial park in the Southeast. The tradition of quality and excellence established by Webb is being carried on by his sons, Bill, Jr. and Dan.

Dan graduated with a Master of Engineering degree from the University of Florida. After graduation Dan joined Caudill Rowlett and Scott in Houston, Texas, which gave him the opportunity to design industrial, institutional, and airport buildings around the world. However, Dan and Bill credit their father with teaching them about the development business and entrepreneurial spirit.

The William C. Webb family has developed three of Florida Trends top ten ranked industrial parks, as well as hundreds of buildings for manufacturing, distribution, and offices.

Webb began the development of Miami's landmark Sunshine State Industrial Park in the mid 1950s, long before environmental planning, landscaping, or green belt areas in industrial development became fashionable. The 330 acre industrial park pioneered a fresh

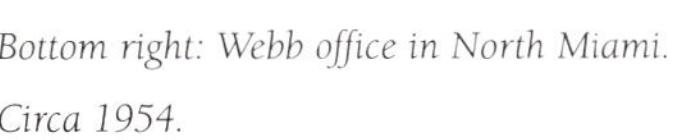

Bottom right: Webb office in North Miami. Circa 1954.

Bottom left: Remington College of Nursing. Circa 2008.

approach to industrial planning and remains a major industrial park in the Miami area. The 110 foot high arch of industry is a South Florida landmark.

The 1,500 acre Imeson International Industrial Park in Jacksonville is perfectly positioned to serve local, regional, national, and international markets from one of the fastest-growing areas of the Sunbelt. The park is served by six major highways, CSX Rail, and the Ports of Jacksonville and serves a diverse mix of international, national, and local manufacturers and distributors. We currently have 7,300,000 square feet of building space in the park and have development rights for 18,500,000 square feet. In 2008, we completed a design-build-leaseback for Samsonite Corp's new 817,000 square foot state-of-the-art distribution center for the US.

The Airport Industrial Park at Orlando was the largest single project undertaken by William C. Webb family. The master-planned commercial mixed-use park is adjacent to Orlando International Airport, only six miles from downtown Orlando, and less than an hour from the Kennedy Space Center. Webb provided the master planning of the park and coordinated the installation of the infrastructure on behalf of the owners. We made the effort to preserve the beauty of the national environment through careful planning and land management to make the Airport International Park at Orlando, as its known today, a showcase international park.

Florida Crown Development Corp. is the parent to the operating companies; William C. Webb Company, which is a general contractor providing industrial/commercial construction; Florida Crown Architects, Engineers, & Planners, Inc., involved in architectural design and engineering; Webb International, Inc., a licensed real estate broker; and Imeson Distribution Center, Inc., a public warehousing company.

Because of their unmatched depth of experience and stability, Florida Crown Development Corp. subsidiaries can provide a unique, full-service capability that includes creating major master-planned industrial parks featuring a complete range of sale, lease, and sale/leaseback options. The firm also provides fast-track, design-build services for turnkey, custom-built office, warehousing, distribution, and manufacturing facilities. Our primary mission is to provide design-build-leaseback facilities on our properties in the State of Florida. However, we have provided design-build services throughout the US for our customers.

Florida Crown Development Corp. and subsidiaries are headquartered in Orlando at 3600 Vineland Road.

Above: Dan Webb at the State Emergency Response Center. Circa 2007.

Below: GE Appliance Distribution Center. Circa 1987.

Orlando Utilities Commission

Reliability is a way of life at OUC—The Reliable One. Year after year, OUC and its dedicated employees are recognized for delivering outstanding service and the highest reliability.

Orlando Utilities Commission, better known as OUC–The Reliable One, has some of the lowest rates in the state, the best reliability, cleanest water, a strong environmental record and high customer satisfaction level.

Central Florida's hometown utility is the second largest municipal utility in Florida, providing electric and water services to more than 254,000 customers in Orlando, St. Cloud and portions of unincorporated Orange and Osceola Counties.

OUC's history dates from 1922, when the city of Orlando bought Orlando Water & Light Company, a privately held company that had been in operation since 1901. City leaders issued $975,000 in bonds to purchase and improve the utility.

In 1923 the State Legislature granted the city a charter to establish the Orlando Utilities Commission to operate the system. After voters approved $575,000 in additional bonds to expand the utility, OUC built a new, larger plant—the Lake Ivanhoe Power and Water Plant on North Orange Avenue, which is now a performing arts center.

Orlando's initial $1.55 million investment has grown into an electric and water utility with more than $2 billion in assets and annual operating revenues in excess of $763 million. Total electric sales have soared from 7 million kilowatt hours to nearly 8 trillion per year. Likewise, water sales have risen from less than 700,000 gallons per year to 30 billion gallons per year.

To keep up with growth, OUC has built and expanded power and water plants, all financed with bonds covered by its own revenues. At the same time, OUC has consistently maintained double-A bond ratings, among the best given by financial analysts.

The utility annually returns to its owners–the citizens of the city of Orlando–payments that make up a sizable portion of the city's general fund and help pay for police and fire services, parks and recreation.

OUC has always excelled at providing customers with reliable, affordable power while building its power plants with the best available environmental controls at the time of construction. OUC's Curtis H. Stanton Energy Center in east Orange County is a strategically phased "powerhouse" comprising a portfolio of clean, modern, fuel-diverse and environmentally sound power generation equipment with state-of-the-art pollution controls and a gross capacity of 1,523 megawatts.

Stanton Units 1 and 2 are among the most environmentally sound coal-burning operations in the nation, meeting or surpassing all federal and state environmental limits for air emissions. Stanton A, a natural gas-fired combined cycle unit, also uses the most efficient and environmentally sensitive fossil-fueled technology available. To help meet future generation needs, OUC is scheduled to bring a 300-megawatt combined cycle plant online in 2010.

This diverse portfolio includes a successful landfill gas partnership between OUC and Orange County that has been turning trash into treasure for the past decade, producing more than 100,000 megawatt hours of reduced emissions power annually.

OUC also has the highest reliability in the region. In comparison data, OUC routinely tops the state's investor-owned utilities in

overall electric reliability and performance, and OUC is a four-time winner of the PA Consulting Group's ReliabilityOne™ award in the Southeast region, given annually to the utility that excels in delivering reliable electric service to customers.

From advanced ozone purification systems to state-of-the-art water testing facilities, OUC provides customers with clean, safe, great tasting water. Water is drawn from the lower Floridan aquifer and treated with ozone, the strongest disinfectant available. OUC is dramatically reducing the use of chlorine in its water system and removing hydrogen sulfide, a naturally occurring compound that can create an unpleasant taste and odor in water. The result is tap water that tastes so good it bears the company's name–H2OUC.

OUC is committed to protecting this valuable resource and working with local and regional partners to drive customer education while promoting the development of alternative water resources and a regional water picture.

Recognizing the unmet needs of large commercial customers, OUC has ventured into several new business directions, including OUCooling and OUConvenient Lighting. OUCooling, which provides chilled water for air conditioning, operates six chilled water plants in four chilled water districts with more than 30,000 tons of cooling capacity. OUConvenient Lighting provides innovative outdoor lighting solutions throughout Central Florida.

OUC's customer service center will be "The Greenest Building in Downtown" when it opens in 2008. Designed to meet Gold LEED (Leadership in Energy and Environmental Design) Certification, the building will feature a two-thousand-square-foot solar array and a solar hot water system as well as high efficiency windows, low-flow water fixtures and a storm water collection system for irrigation.

OUC's employees and customers are deeply involved in dozens of community projects each year. In 2007, OUC and its customers marked the $1 million milestone in donations to Project CARE, the utility's emergency bill payment assistance program. Since the program began more than $1,025,602 in assistance has been provided to 5,397 families in need.

Among the many other organizations that have benefited from OUC's volunteer efforts are Second Harvest Food Bank, March of Dimes, Seniors First (Meals on Wheels), Juvenile Diabetes, CrimeLine, and Junior Achievement.

For additional information about OUC–The Reliable One, visit www.ouc.com.

Above: The Stanton Energy Center, located in east Orange County, is a strategically phased powerhouse comprising a portfolio of clean, modern and fuel diverse power generation equipment and featuring state-of-the-art environmental protection equipment.

Below: OUC is dedicated to providing clean, great tasting water to customers today, while also leading the search for innovative, reliable sources of water that will serve Central Florida for generations to come.

J. Rolfe Davis Insurance

Joseph Rolfe Davis was born on February 11, 1904 and was a native of Granger County, Tennessee. He was educated at Tennessee secondary schools and attended Carson Newman College. After college, an office supply house in Knoxville employed him. Davis was presented with an offer from George Bannister to relocate to Florida.

At age twenty-one, Davis came to Orlando with only twenty-five dollars to his name. In 1928, he partnered with Bannister to form the Davis and Bannister Office Equipment Company. This partnership continued for three years when Davis left and started the Davis Office Supply Company. When the office supply company was well established and growing on its own, he sold the company and purchased the Woods W. Rogers Jr. Insurance Agency, later to become the J. Rolfe Davis Insurance Agency.

His care and concern for the community was the driving force behind everything he did. With the goal of improving the city of Orlando, Davis ran for mayor and on October 15, 1952, he made headlines by winning the mayoral election with 5,273 votes. The forty-nine year old received more votes than all three opponents combined. During his term as mayor, he concentrated on stabilizing the city's financial picture. His fiscal policies enabled Orlando to increase road development including Interstate 4 and a causeway later dedicated in his honor.

Above: J. Rolfe Davis is the second person from the left.

As mayor, Davis would always carry $100 in his pocket. He did not believe in taking more than $100 donation from his constituents because if they ever asked him to do something that he did not believe in, he would simply return the donation. The guiding principles of his life were integrity, fairness and honor.

Clearly, Davis was very involved in the community, holding positions such as president of the Kiwanis, county commissioner, president of the Orlando Chamber of Commerce, corporate director for Sun Banks of Florida, president of the Country Club of Orlando, and a member of the Florida State Road Board.

J. Rolfe married the former Jeannette Griffin of Kissimmee and was the father of two children, Jeanne Marie and J. Rolfe Jr. Davis was very patriotic and spearheaded USO's during World War II. He was a devout Presbyterian, enjoyed raising orchids and playing golf. In 1988, Davis died at the age of eighty-four.

Davis left a legacy of an enduring respect for tradition. Following his lead, the agency has distinguished itself by setting the highest standard of service. The company's resources are focused on customized business solutions and are committed to exceeding client's expectations.

J. Rolfe Davis Insurance is in its third generation of providing complete risk management and business consulting services including commercial property and casualty, employee benefits, personal insurance and financial strategy. Davis' son-in-law, Marion Hatcher purchased the agency in the late 1960s and continued to build the business. In the early 1970s, Hatcher hired a group of young men to sell insurance under his guidance and direction. This group including Monty McBryde, John Watson, Donald Boone, Kipp Minter and David McKinney purchased the company from Hatcher in the mid 1980s. The current ownership group includes Donald Boone, David McKinney, and Bruce Arrow, as well as a large number of their employees.

The agency is ranked among the top 100 largest brokers in the U.S. by *Business Insurance Magazine*, is among the top 100 privately held insurance agencies in the country and was chosen as an Agency of the Year by National Underwriter Magazine. J. Rolfe Davis Insurance has also been selected one of *Orlando Sentinel*'s "Top 100 Companies for Working Families" each year since 2005.

The employee-owned organization has grown to more than 130 employees serving the nation's most prestigious businesses and families. This team of insurance, benefits and risk management specialists deliver a full array of value-added services. Their knowledge and expertise has earned them the status of a trusted advisor with their clients. They have earned that status by focusing their goal of creating customized solutions specific to the needs of their clients. With a team of specialists implementing programs as distinctly individual as a company trademark.

For over sixty-five years, J. Rolfe Davis Insurance has been immersed in the community. They are proud that their gift giving has extended to more than eighty charities, schools and community-based groups. The employees of J. Rolfe Davis have supported the American Cancer Society, Heart of Florida United Way, Second Harvest Food Bank and the Muscular Dystrophy Association.

The agency supports faith-based initiatives including the Good Samaritan Fund, the Jewish Federation of Greater Orlando, Fellowship of Christian Athletes, St. John Vianney School and Lake Highland Prep to name a few. From A Gift for Teaching to UCF, the colleagues of J. Rolfe Davis Insurance dig deep to financially support the needs of their community. After Hurricane Katrina, employees donated over $23,000 to the Heart of Florida United Way.

While financial stewardship is important, J. Rolfe Davis employees believe that donation of time is equally, if not more important. This is why you will find employees of J. Rolfe Davis building homes for Habitat for Humanity or donating and wrapping presents for United Cerebral Palsy. JRD employees are at the forefront in giving and therefore sustaining the community they call home.

The J. Rolfe Davis Insurance philosophy concentrates on quality. That philosophy will not change. When clients choose J. Rolfe Davis Insurance, they can be sure they have found their long-term trusted business advisor.

For more information about J. Rolfe Davis Insurance, please visit www.jrdavis.com.

Below: The dedication of the J. Rolfe Davis Causeway, 1958.

Parker Boats

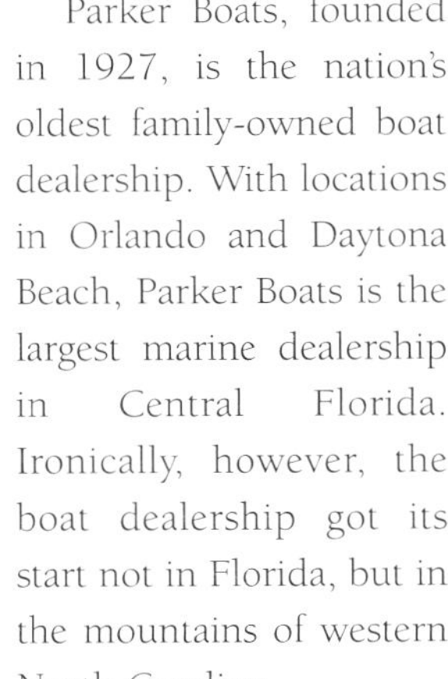

Above: Parker Boats' first location in Ashville, North Carolina.

Below: Roy W. Parker, Sr. and wife Sophie.

Parker Boats, founded in 1927, is the nation's oldest family-owned boat dealership. With locations in Orlando and Daytona Beach, Parker Boats is the largest marine dealership in Central Florida. Ironically, however, the boat dealership got its start not in Florida, but in the mountains of western North Carolina.

The business was founded in 1927 by Roy W. Parker, Sr., an ambitious and industrious young man who grew up in the little mountain town of Candler, North Carolina. Although he had only a sixth-grade education, young Roy was determined to succeed. Packing all his belongings in a shoe box, he followed two other brothers to the nearby city of Asheville. One of the brothers had found work as an A-model Ford mechanic, the other as a bricklayer, and Roy learned both trades before turning his attention to the boat business.

Parker got his start racing boats, later building a boat racing course on Lake Lure in the North Carolina mountains. He also operated a boat rental concession on Fontana Lake and an Asheville municipal lake, and operated a sightseeing boat to the Fontana dam and back. Parker also worked as a salesman for a local Cadillac dealer, who allowed him to display his boats in the auto showroom.

Parker also had a retail store in Ashville, North Carolina where, to help make ends meet, he and his family lived in a small apartment on the second floor.

His industriousness caught the attention of a Johnson Motors representative who offered him a dealership in Orlando. Parker opened the dealership on West Church Street in 1939, a location he shared with a motorcycle shop.

From 1939 to 1949, Parker divided his time between Florida and North Carolina, selling boats in Orlando in the winter and renting and selling boats on the mountain lakes in the summer. Finally deciding that his future was in Florida, Parker moved to Orlando full-time in 1949.

Parker purchased a small service station and trailer park on North Orange Avenue and started a boat business called Orlando Outdoor Marine. The businesses slow-but-steady growth led to a major expansion of the Orange Avenue location in 1952. At the same time, the company name was changed to Parker Boats.

Parker's wife, Sophie, was very involved in the business, serving as secretary/treasurer and keeping the books. "She's the one who kept things going," explains her son, Roy Parker, Jr. "She was the one you had to go through if you wanted any money."

At the time, the dealership specialized in Chris Craft boats, most of which were made of wood. Some of the boats came as kits and had to be assembled on site or by the customer.

Roy, Jr., who now serves as president of Parker Boats, joined the business in 1964 and his two brothers, David and Bruce, entered the firm in the early 1970s. The two younger brothers were later bought out by Roy, Jr.

Although the firm suffered a big downturn during the oil embargo of the 1979, losing half their business almost overnight, the Parkers managed to hold on and rebound once economic conditions improved.

Roy, Sr. died in 1990 but remained active in the business until the end. "We fixed him up with his own comfortable office at our new location and he came in right up until the day before he died," his son recalls. Sophie, now ninety-five, retired many years ago.

Parker Boats moved to its present location at 455 South Lake Destiny Road in 1985, a move that helped the firm increase business by 150 percent during the first year in the new building. A second location was opened in Daytona Beach in 2007.

Parker Boats now has about fifty employees at the two locations and is a full-service marine dealer, offering maintenance, repair and service, in addition to sales and brokerage. The service department is one of the few to have three master technicians on staff.

The dealership offers Sea Ray boats, the largest seller in the nation, as well as highly respected Boston Whaler boats. Parker Boats has been recognized as a Sea Ray Ambassador dealer for its consistently high customer satisfaction (CSI) scores and has also earned similar recognition from Mercury Marine.

The third generation is now becoming active in the business. Brad Parker serves as manager of the Daytona Beach location, and his brother, Bobby, works in sales at the Orlando location and serves as general manager of the brokerage division.

After more than eighty years in business, Parker Boats has become one of the largest and most respected dealerships in the Southeast and looks forward to many more successful years in the future.

Additional information is available on the Internet at www.parkerboats.com.

Above: Original location on Orange Avenue in Orlando.

Below: Current Orlando location, 455 South Lake Destiny Road.

M. D. Anderson Cancer Center Orlando

M. D. Anderson Cancer Center Orlando opened in January 1991 as a cooperative effort between the University of Texas, M. D. Anderson Cancer Center and Orlando Regional Healthcare. The Orlando facility was the first affiliate of the renowned cancer center outside Texas.

The mission statement of the center is: "To use every available resource to defeat cancer."

The M. D. Anderson Cancer Center in Houston, Texas has long been recognized as a world leader in innovative technology, cancer research, education, prevention and treatment, and this collaborative effort extended the center's expertise to residents of Florida and the Southeastern United States.

Known originally as the Orlando Cancer Center, the facility opened with nine physicians, including four radiation oncologists and five medical oncologists, one of whom also served as a part-time medical director.

The center grew rapidly because of the scope and quality of care available through the affiliation with M. D. Anderson Cancer Center, and the name was changed to M. D. Anderson Cancer Center Orlando in 1994. By 2007 the staff grew to 50 physicians and a support staff of 375.

Based on the number of cases reported to the Florida Cancer Data Base, M. D. Anderson-Orlando is the second largest cancer center in Florida. According to the most recent annual statistics, more than 4,200 new patients register each year with the cancer center. Breast cancer is the most common cancer treated at the center, followed by prostate, lung cancer, colon/rectal cancer, and melanoma.

Above: Charles Lewis Pavilion, home of M. D. Anderson Cancer Center Orlando.

Below: Dr. Baker, Cancer research-discoveries from bench to bedside.

As patients flocked to M. D. Anderson-Orlando, it soon became apparent that a larger facility was needed. In 1997 former President George Bush and the staff of M. D. Anderson-Orlando broke ground for a new state-of-the-art facility named the Charles Lewis Pavilion. In 2003, staff and patients moved into the new 10-story, 220,000-square-foot facility at 1400 South Orange Avenue in downtown Orlando.

The Charles Lewis Pavilion houses the majority of the services provided by M. D. Anderson-Orlando and consists of 150 private inpatient beds, an ambulatory treatment center capable of treating 150 to 200 patients each day, a radiation oncology department capable of treating 180 patients daily, a laboratory, medical oncology and gynecologic oncology clinics and physician offices, surgical specialty clinics, and a clinical research department. Also included are facilities for cancer risk analysis and genetic counseling, pharmacies for chemotherapy admixing and retail sales, a conference and telemedicine center, and spaces for psychosocial and spiritual support services. A patient and family learning center, professional library, business offices, and administrative offices are also included in the facility.

The Charles Lewis Plaza consists of the Kobrin Gardens, an outdoor plaza for respite and relaxation. A Labyrinth embedded in the

outdoor plaza is used for meditation and reflection, a part of the Mind, Body, Spirit Institute at the center.

In 2005 the Cancer Research Institute, under M. D. Anderson-Orlando, was established and a ten-thousand-square-foot facility dedicated to basic and translational cancer research was opened on the campus. Within eighteen months, five PhD research scientists and a team of research assistants were involved with research projects relating to cancer biology, radiation biology, and nano-biology and nearly $1 million in grants and philanthropic funds were raised to support these very productive projects.

Clinical research is a high priority of M. D. Anderson-Orlando and clinical trials are offered by the parent institution in Houston and by national cooperative research groups. Industry-sponsored and investigator initiated trials are also utilized. More than 150 patients are entered into clinical trails each year.

Education is also an important commitment at M. D. Anderson-Orlando. In addition to patient and community-based educational programs, the center started the first fellowship program in hematology and medical oncology in Central Florida and will train six physicians who have completed their internal medicine residency in these cancer and blood disease oriented specialties.

Advanced technologies have also received major attention at the center. In the radiation oncology department, two of the most technologically advanced instruments for the treatment of cancer have been installed in the new cancer center, housed within the Charles Lewis Pavilion. The Novalis Shaped Beam Surgery system and the Helical Tomotherapy unit allows for the most precise delivery of radiation therapy to patients minimizing radiation exposure to surrounding normal tissue. The center is opening a proton therapy unit in 2009. Medical physics is staffed by ten PhD trained physicists, including several enrolled in the physics residency program.

In 2007, for the fourth time in six years, *U.S. News & World Report* ranked M. D. Anderson Cancer Center in Houston as the top cancer treatment hospital in the United States and one of the top two cancer hospitals for the past seventeen years.

Also in 2007, for the seventh year in succession, M. D. Anderson Cancer Center Orlando was named the "Best Cancer Center in Florida" by Florida Magazine.

At M. D. Anderson Cancer Center Orlando, our mission is simple—to eliminate cancer. Achieving this goal begins with integrated programs in cancer treatment, clinical trials, education programs, and cancer prevention.

To us, people are more important than just their cancer symptoms. Compassion–along with innovative cancer treatment, cutting-edge cancer research, comprehensive education and research-based prevention of both common and rare cancers—has earned the gratitude of countless adult and pediatric cancer patients and their families.

Above: Cancer therapies—curing more patients and improving the quality of life.

Below: Minimally invasive surgery—more accepting to patients.

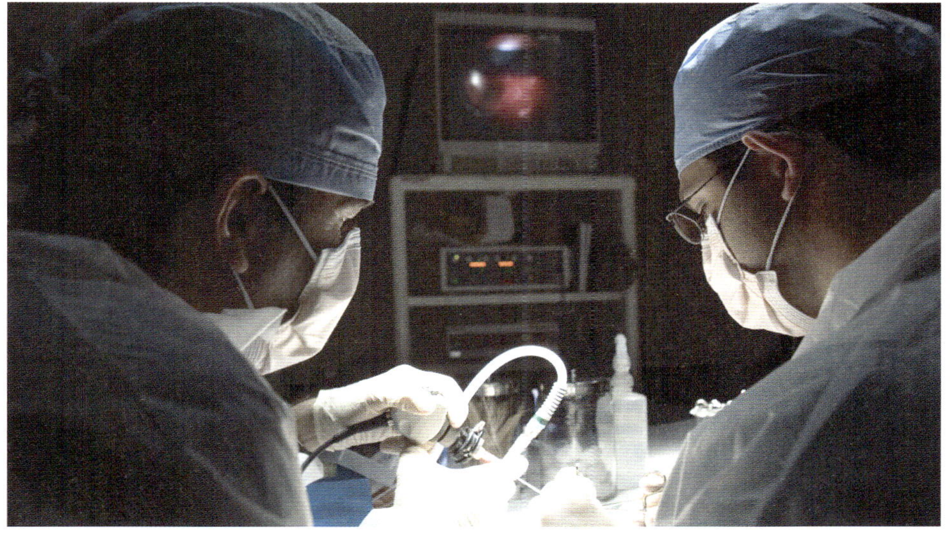

Daniels Manufacturing Corporation

Above: DMC has three employees who originally worked in Michigan. Left to right: George Daniels, John D. Eby and Karl Stommel.

Below: DMC is located at 506 Thorpe Road in Orlando, Florida.

With experience that spans more than five decades, Daniels Manufacturing Corporation is the recognized leader in the aircraft and aerospace tool industry. Products of the Orlando-based manufacturer have been used on virtually every defense system, aircraft program, land or sea-going transport system, as well as in the space exploration program.

DMC was founded by William A. Daniels and began operation as a machine shop in Michigan in the early 1950s. In those early days, the firm specialized in close tolerance machining of blast tubes for the solid rocket Nike Missile System, which protected American cities from possible enemy nuclear bomber attacks.

During a visit to a Convair plant in Fort Worth, Texas during the 1950s, Daniels was asked if his firm could build a 'crimp tool'. Although Daniels had never heard of a crimp tool, he accepted the challenge. By the late 1950s, DMC had begun to develop its own line of wire crimp tools and other accessory tooling for the assembly of crimp type electrical connectors.

In 1968, George Daniels, son of founder William A. Daniels, chose Orlando as his base of operations to sell DMC products on the east coast. DMC began manufacturing operations in Orlando in 1972 as Balmar Enterprises, Inc. The original location was a rented facility on Palm Ridge Way, where the company operated a machine shop and warehouse. Soon after moving to Orlando, the corporate name was changed to Balmar Crimp Tool Corp.

Three DMC employees who originally worked for the firm in Michigan, George Daniels, John D. Eby and Karl Stommel, are still employed by the firm. In addition, DMC has six employees who have been with the company for more than thirty years. Dave Eby has been with the company forty-five years; George Daniels, forty years; Dave Kelly and Ralph Recht for thirty-four years; Blaise Figura, thirty-three years; and Bill Kirk, thirty-two years.

DMC expanded its Orlando operation over the years and moved to Anno Avenue in the late 1970s. In 1983, DMC closed its Michigan facility and continued its expansion in Orlando. DMC moved into its present facility 526 Thorpe Road in 1991 where it continues to produce its line of wire crimp tools and electrical connector accessory tooling.

Today, DMC is a leader in tool systems and technology for the aerospace, military and telecommunications industries. DMC is a major supplier to the users of aircraft and military type electrical connectors. Almost all non-Eastern bloc jet aircraft flying anywhere in the free world were assembled using DMC tools.

DMC has developed a worldwide network of professionals to aid in answering technical questions, designing new service kits, modifying existing kits, and processing orders for complete kits and individual components.

The company works continually with the government and major manufacturers in the development of new products and support materials to keep pace with the most recent developments in technology.

DMC Aircraft Tool Kits provide complete capability for maintenance and production applications. The kits have all the tools and information required to support an entire aircraft wiring system.

DMC also produces a complete line of adapter tools and torque tools, an extensive line of manual, pneumatic, and hydraulic tools and accessories used to crimp contacts and terminals onto power and coaxial conductors, and metal and plastic tools specially designed to remove contacts from electrical connectors.

Other DMC products include Safe-T-Cable™, the complete fastener retention system, wire crimp pull testers, wire strippers and other tools.

Complete in-factory repair and recalibration services are provided for all products manufactured by DMC.

DMC maintains an online store featuring more than seventy-six hundred of its most popular products. An online catalog is also available at www.dmctools.com.

DMC is dedicated to continually acquiring the most modern production machinery and implementing the latest cutting-edge technology in order to keep itself highly competitive in an ever-more-challenging world.

Above: Today DMC is a major supplier to the users of aircraft and military type electrical connectors.

The Florida Hotel & Conference Center

Following an extensive $25-million renovation, The Florida Hotel and Conference Center at the Florida Mall now offers an unmatched blend of luxurious comfort and world-class service in the heart of all that Orlando has to offer.

Originally an Adams Mark Hotel, the property was purchased in 2004 by a group headed by Terry Shaikh, who serves as president of the company. The new owners decided the hotel was in need of major renovation and undertook a complete overhaul that transformed the hotel into a beautiful, modern, state-of-the-art facility.

The hotel remained fully operational during the renovations, despite three major hurricanes.

Described as "the friendliest hotel in Orlando," The Florida Hotel and Conference Center is conveniently located at the Florida Mall at 1500 Sand Lake Road in Orlando. The main goal of the new owners is to be a local community hotel for Orlando. The aim is to grow by word of mouth, become the employer everyone wishes to work for, and the hotel where everybody wants to stay.

The hotel has three hundred employees and strongly believes that if it takes good care of its employees, they will take good care of the guests. Management believes strongly that employee retention is its number one goal.

The Florida Hotel and Conference Center provides more than fifty thousand square feet of meeting space, making it the ideal location

for meetings and conventions, weddings and social events, and leisure or business travel. The hotel's knowledgeable sales and catering team will be happy to help make your Orlando meeting a huge success.

The hotel offers 511 newly renovated guest rooms with the latest in high-tech amenities and the comfort of plush pillowtop beds. Exceptional amenities include a restaurant, refrigerators and thirty-two inch wall-mounted, flat panel televisions in each room and many other features, such as Starbucks and the Florida Mall.

Guests may enjoy a heated pool and spa, in-room spa treatments, and a Starbucks Coffee Shop. Regularly scheduled transportation to Disney attractions is provided free.

A Business Center at The Florida Hotel and Conference Center is available during business hours to provide pre-convention printing, copying, faxing, typing assistance, equipment rentals and shipping. Computer workstations with printer and Internet connections are available twenty-four hours per day, along with laptop connections to printers and Internet access.

The Florida Hotel and Conference Center is conveniently located on Sand Lake Road and is connected with the Florida Mall, which

offers fabulous fashion, exceptional eateries and delightful diversions. The Mall features Dillard's, JCPenney, Macy's, Nordstrom, Saks Fifth Avenue, and Sears, along with more than 250 specialty stores.

With a complete renovation and expansion completed in November 1999, the Florida Mall boasts over fifty new specialty retailers, including twenty-five making their Central Florida debut.

The hotel's central location places guests only minutes from Disney World, Sea World, and Universal Studios. The hotel's central location—midway between Orlando International Airport and Disney World—is also convenient to the Orange County Convention Center. And, because Orlando is located in the central part of Florida, Daytona, the Tampa Bay area, and the Space Coast beaches are just a short drive from the hotel.

Whether you are coming to Orlando for business or vacation, The Florida Hotel and Conference Center has all the comfort and amenities to make your stay a pleasure.

For complete details on The Florida Hotel & Conference Center, please visit www.thefloridahotelorlando.com.

Amazon Hose & Rubber Company

When Harry Jacoby founded Amazon Hose & Rubber Company in 1919, virtually all hose was made of pure rubber. The primary source for most of the rubber was the Amazon River Basin of South America, so Jacoby adopted the name "Amazon" for his new company.

Jacoby, with only a sixth-grade education but a larger-than-life personality, was a classic entrepreneur who bought military surplus lots of hose that sometimes included can openers, boots, and nurse's uniforms—establishing Amazon's initial inventory.

The business began in Chicago but Jacoby moved to Miami in 1947 to dabble in race horses and escape the Chicago winters. The company is now headquartered in Orlando, with branches in Miami, Tampa, and Chicago.

Amazon Hose & Rubber maintains a vast inventory of quality hose and coupling products, ranging from pressure washer, agricultural, chemical hoses to gaskets, quick-disconnect couplings, and concrete and industrial fittings. The company prides itself on supplying expert service and solving problems.

Jacoby died in 1973 and his wife, Rene, had to fight with a bank for control of the company. At the time, the bank did not feel a woman could handle the responsibilities of a CEO in a male-dominated industry. However, Rene, who always used her initials to conceal the fact that she was a woman, began a three-generation tradition of female leadership of the company.

Above: Gale Jacoby Petronis as a teenager posing for an advertising campaign.

Below: The Orlando Amazon headquarters opened in 1981 on the corner of Princeton and Orange Blossom Trail. The Amazon Rain Forest mural was added in 2001. courtesy of chip riggs.

Rene Jacoby, who remained active in the firm until her death at the age of ninety, was succeeded as CEO by her daughter, Gale Petronis. Gale semi-retired in 2005 and was succeeded by her daughter, Summer Rodman.

Other family members have also been involved in the company, including Kenny Niedhamer, Rene's brother, who worked until he was ninety-one. Kenny was noted for his photographic memory and was reputed to know the inventory of every hose and fitting in stock without looking it up.

Besides family members, Amazon's growth through the years is due largely to key employees. A total of eighteen employees have been with the company fifteen years or longer.

Bill Smith became general manager of all stores in 2000, the same year Amazon broke $10 million in sales, and a managerial infrastructure was developed with branch managers and warehouse managers in each store.

Bill "Hippy" Hippenmeir, a hydraulic supervisor at Amazon's Tampa location, has been with the company since the 1970s and feels its success is the result of using the "Golden Rule" as the foundation for customer service.

"I love to watch the eyes of our warehouse technicians light up when they discover a solution to a problem that a customer had thought unsolvable," says Hippenmeir. "Even more, I love to watch the eyes and smile of the customer who leaves our building with their problem resolved."

For more information about Amazon Hose & Rubber Company and its servicees, please visit www.amazonhose.com.

Lambert Corporation

For more than fifty years, Lambert Corporation has produced quality construction chemicals used by the national and international concrete construction industry. Lambert products were utilized in a number of well known Orange County construction projects; including Disney World, Amway Arena, Sun Trust Tower, and many downtown Orlando landmarks.

Lambert Corporation offers liquid latex adhesives, concrete resurfacing and patching products, liquid surface sealers and coatings, dry power pigments for coloring cement and mortar, concrete hardeners and many other products. Many of these products can be used in work related to concrete, precast and other portland cement systems.

Charles Lambert founded Lambert Corporation in Houston, Texas in 1945 and the Orlando plant was opened in 1953. Lambert sold both plant operations to Guardsman Chemical in 1970 and the company operated as a subsidiary of Guardsman until 1978, when it was purchased by Roger Meyer and two partners. The partners retired from the company in the late 1980s and the company is now owned by Steven Meyer, son of Roger.

Lambert Corporation has operated under the same name and in the same location for thirty years. Corporate headquarters and a manufacturing plant are located in downtown Orlando at 20 North Coburn Avenue.

The company has gone through a number of important changes since it was purchased by Roger, beginning with an industry change that targeted the building chemicals market. In 1999 the second generation manager, Steven, purchased the business from his father and continued the processes which led to previous successes.

Along with Vice President Steve Kuhle, Meyer has continued with product development and marketing, along with improved manufacturing equipment that has allowed for mass production. Such equipment includes silos used for resurfacing products that were purchased five years ago.

Lambert Corporation employs twenty-five individuals. The current customer focus targets the ready-mix concrete producers, precast concrete producers, and the construction supply industries. The company has seen positive growth of ten to twenty percent each year, more than doubling corporate revenues since 1999.

Currently, Lambert Corporation is in the design stages of a new manufacturing facility to be located in the Orlando area. Meyer, along with Kuhle and another partner, have purchased a sister company, Alpha Manufacturing, which will aid in the manufacturing processes faced by Lambert. Lambert's management feels these developments, along with product diversification, private labeling investments and adaptability will lead to continued controlled growth both nationally and internationally.

Employees of Lambert Corporation are active in the community, making continuous donations to various U.S. military veteran support groups, local sports teams and schools, and numerous political agencies and officials.

Lambert Corporation maintains an information rich, easily navigable website at www.lambertusa.com.

Lambert Corporation over fifty years of experience in the construction industry.

UCF Federal Credit Union

The credit union movement began more than 150 years ago, while the first U.S. credit union was established in the early 1900s. UCF Federal Credit Union was founded in 1971 to serve the faculty and staff of what was then Florida Technology University, now the University of Central Florida.

Of course, in 1971 the area surrounding FTU was quite different from the vibrant business and population center now radiating from the UCF hub on Alafaya Trail. What once were pastures and piney woods with pristine sandy-bottom lakes, with only a few small businesses and very few homes within five miles, has become a lively epicenter of homes, apartments and businesses of every size and description.

Keeping pace with the university, UCF Federal has grown from a box in a drawer to a beautiful new administrative center in the Central Florida Research Park, with three additional convenient branch offices. Under the guidance of selfless, volunteer Board Members like Jim Smith, Barth Engert, Naval Modani and all of the current Board of Directors, UCF Federal strives to meet all of its members' needs for financial services.

As our members know, the critical difference between a bank and a credit union is that a bank is in business to make a profit. At a credit union, on the other hand, the members are the shareholders and profits are returned to members as dividends, competitive loan rates and low-cost or no-cost services. The National Credit Union Share Insurance Fund insures deposits up to $100,000, with additional coverage for Individual Retirement Accounts (IRAs).

Membership in UCF Federal is open to employees, faculty, students, and alumni of UCF; Booster Club members; Central Florida Research Park employees; and the immediate families of all members. In addition, if a member of your family meets any of these criteria–even if they are not a credit union member–you are eligible to join the Credit Union. We can also help you become a Booster at our offices, which automatically qualifies you for credit union membership.

UCF Federal takes pride in its ability and desire to deliver professional service in a

personal way. Since credit union staff works for the members, our personalized service shines through every day. In keeping with the credit union philosophy of "People Helping People," members receive personal attention, professional service, and genuine appreciation every time they visit the Credit Union.

You may establish membership with us by opening a Share (savings) account with a minimum deposit of $50 and a small membership fee. UCF Federal offers a variety of checking and savings accounts, including money markets, certificates, and IRA accounts and easy access through ATM/debit cards.

Loan services available from the Credit Union include home mortgages; auto, motorcycle, RV, and boat loans; first-time homebuyer's down payment assistance programs; home equity loans; land loans, construction loans, personal loans, and several MasterCard options with low, fixed interest rates.

Other membership perks include worldwide ATM access, free checking, drive-thru banking, free online banking with BillPay and hassle-free car buying services.

The main office of UCF Federal Credit Union is located at 12253 Challenger Parkway in Orlando and the campus office is located across from Barnes & Noble at the center of the UCF campus. We also maintain a student-run branch at Timber Creek High School. A new branch will open across from UCF in the University Commons in 2008.

The Credit Union is committed to helping people satisfy their individual financial needs. That is what a credit union is all about—confidential, professional service. At UCF Federal, "People Helping People" is not just a catchy slogan, it is a philosophy we put into practice every day.

Grosvenor Building Services, Inc.

Grosvenor Building Services, Inc. was founded in 1959 when John Bernard McCauley returned to Ireland after a tour with the U.S. Army. With only his bicycle for transportation, McCauley and his wife, Rita, started a small window cleaning business. Today, the commercial cleaning company operates on two continents with more than 5,000 employees.

Grosvenor's U.S. operation was organized in 1983 and is headquartered in Orlando. The U.S. operation, which also has offices in Georgia and Mississippi, employs 700 persons and is managed by Rita McCauley, daughter of founder's John Bernard and Rita McCauley.

Rita McCauley's brother, Bernard, runs the operation in Ireland and her brother Ben, runs the operation in the United Kingdom, and she explains that the business has been a family affair from the companies earliest days in Belfast, when her Uncle Leo helped grow the business. In more modern times, her brothers Desmond and Gabriel, and her sister Barbara have played a part in shaping the companies future.

"My father was born on Grosvenor Road in Belfast and the name Grosvenor is synonymous with quality and strength, so we picked it for a company name," she explains.

Grosvenor Cleaning Services are more than cleaning specialists. Each day, the company is responsible for maintaining clean working and service environments in large office complexes, shopping centers, and industrial sites worldwide.

"We believe in serving the client and will sit down and work out exactly the building cleaning requirements required," says McCauley. She adds that the company has the expertise, efficient and well-trained staff, and sophisticated equipment and materials to fulfill any assignment.

Grosvenor provides services to all sectors of the business community, including commercial offices, retail establishments, medical hospitals and clinics, airports, tourist attractions, industrial and manufacturing plants, and government facilities.

The mission of Grosvenor Building Services is to be an industry leader in providing premier facility services to its customers through the highest level of customer service, commitment to quality and excellence, innovative solutions that promote the needs of customers and the environment, and by adding value and competitiveness.

Grosvenor understands the importance of a "green" work atmosphere and is an industry leader in focusing on cleaning for a better environment.

Good business, according to McCauley, includes partnering with quality vendors and suppliers, as well as establishing memberships in various service organizations like the Chamber of Commerce. The company also supports such community organizations as the Center for Drug Free Living, Midnight Basketball, Grandma's House, and CARE.

Above: Founder John McCauley during his tour with the U.S. Army.

Below: Left to right, Ben McCauley, Co-founder Rita McCauley and Founders Rita and Bernard McCauley.

Hall Brothers Roofing, Inc.

The goal of Hall Brothers Roofing is "to give you peace of mind that your roof is watertight and will withstand all types of weather." This goal has guided the company for more than twenty years and their reputation has established them as one of the leading roofing companies in the Central Florida area.

Hall Brothers Roofing's attention to detail results in beautiful craftsmanship with rows of tile, perfectly even, hip and valleys straight and parallel and perfect mud work. The final products look like works of art.

The company began in 1986 and the name came from the Hall brothers, Don and Randy. In 1992, Randy and his wife left to begin their own company. Don and his wife, Jeannine, continued under the Hall Brothers name. Under Jeannine's supervision, Hall Brothers has continued to grow and now has about 60 employees who installed more than 350 roofs in 2007.

"What makes this company different is that the owners have a staff and crews that are not only talented, but take a great deal of pride in their jobs and their craftsmanship," says company spokesperson Sharon Trump. "Our office staff, superintendents and installation crews have all been with us for many years, and customer satisfaction is number one with each of us."

Jeannine Hall adds that, "The majority of our customers are repeat (both builders and homeowners) and from referrals by other family members. As we have grown larger, we still maintain a personal touch with all our customers."

As a full-service roofing specialist, Hall Brothers installs both residential and commercial roofs, including tile, shingle, flat roofs, custom copper roofs and re-roofs. Crews use a quality control checklist which is double checked by field supervisors with more than forty years combined experience. Installers are covered by General Liability and Workers Comp. This protects the customer.

During and after the three devastating hurricanes that hit the Central Florida area in 2004, Hall Brothers' crews worked incredibly long hours to service a public that was desperate for estimates and re-roofs, while the remainder of the staff struggled to keep up with the phone calls.

The company and its employees believe strongly in giving back to their community. For example the company donated labor for two shingle roofs for Habitat for Humanity, and also did the roof for the WFTV Concept Home. Proceeds from the tour of the home went to benefit the Russell Home for Atypical Children. Staff members regularly per-form volunteer work in storm damaged areas such as New Orleans after Hurricane Katrina and tornados in Lady Lake, Florida.

This family owned and operated business will be here in Orlando serving the community and surrounding area now and in the future. It is a company the community can count on for their roofing needs for the long term.

United Trophy Manufacturing, Inc.

Syd Levy founded United Trophy Manufacturing, Inc. in 1968, shortly after moving to Orlando to find relief for his rheumatoid arthritis. He was born in Canada and lived there the first three decades of his life, but his doctor recommended he leave Ontario for a warmer climate.

He was visiting Miami Beach when he met Marianne Vosilla. It was love at first sight. Syd and Marianne married in 1968 and became business—as well as marriage—partners. After looking around Florida, they decided to make Orlando their new home. He had graduated from Central Collegiate in Hamilton, Ontario in 1950 and started his first business selling trophies and team jackets to schools in central Ontario. "In those days there were only four trophy figurines; a male bowler, a female bowler, male victory, and female victory," Syd notes. "Today we have hundreds of different sports figures."

When United Trophy Manufacturing was founded, trophies were available mostly through jewelry and sporting goods stores. Syd decided to make them his specialty and worked until the early hours of the morning, designing his own line of unique trophies and awards.

Syd and Marianne opened the business at 610 North Orange Avenue in downtown Orlando. The central location was great, although the area was a little run down. Some of the tenants in the complex back then were Orlando Beauty Supply, Frank Parker Florist, Howell Typewriter and Shaver Repair, Alcoholics Anonymous, Catholic Sharing Center Thrift Store, Louis Restaurant, Dong A. Oriental Foods, Hindley Air Products, Carlisle Hughs Sporting Goods, Sentinel Classified Advertising and a printing company. United Trophy quickly outgrew its original thousand square foot store and rented neighboring shops as they became available. Eventually, they occupied and purchased the entire nine store complex that was made up of four separate land parcels.

By 1993, the year United Trophy celebrated its twenty-fifth anniversary, Orange Avenue had become really 'uptown'. Surrounded by the remodeled Orlando Sentinel building and a new courthouse, Syd and Marianne decided they needed to update the image of United Trophy.

The renovation brought the nine store spaces together while retaining the original Art Deco architecture. The front overhangs were joined together, windows and doors were standardized, and stucco and paint gave the stores a unified look. Pastel tropical colors and neon outline completed the exterior. The sales showroom, once spread out in three separate stores, was remodeled into one "mega-showroom." This was recognized with the prestigious Downtown Orlando "Gold Brick Award."

The success of United Trophy led to several other ventures, including Sanford's Flea World in 1981, United Advertising Specialties in 1985, Sign World in 1987, and Fun World, a family amusement park adjacent to Flea World, which opened in 1990.

Levy may be best known for Flea World, "the nation's largest flea market under one roof." More than 1,700 vendors gather at the 104-acre site every Friday, Saturday and Sunday to hawk everything from automotive tires to haircuts.

"I love my businesses, I just live it," says Syd, a dynamic promoter who overcame his health problems to be a successful Orlando businessman.

Above: United Trophy Manufacturing prior to 1995.

Below: United Trophy Manufacturing, Inc., now really "uptown." Circa 2008.

BLP Products, Inc.

When Jimmy Johnson won NASCAR's top championship in 2007, his car was equipped with a carburetor manufactured by BLP Products of Orlando. BLP Products has manufactured high quality race engine parts and components for many of the professional race carburetor builders and NASCAR race teams, along with modifying Holley® race carburetors.

BLP also manufactures special components for Holley® Carburetors, along with designing and developing drive components, belt-driven fuel pumps, piston dome oilers and sheet metal valve covers.

BLP Products began in 1965 as a two-man automotive general repair shop named Bo Laws Automotive. By 1970 the small firm had grown to five employees successfully tuning and race-prepping Corvettes and muscle cars. From 1971 until 1990, the company operated as a combination speed and machine shop, specializing in building high performance products and race engines.

"It was an awesome time in American automotive history and I consider myself very fortunate to have experienced those times," comments Bo Laws. "There were very few racing parts available and we had to make many of our own parts."

Laws was very successful in drag racing in the late 1960s and won several NHRA National Events in the Street Eliminator and Pro Stock divisions. This success helped propel the business and in 1983, Laws was elected to the first Southeast Division NHRA Hall of Fame.

Above: Bo Laws in the company's early years.

Below: Bo Laws with employees at the BLP plant.

In addition to his wife, Barbara, and his family, Laws credits his "right-hand man" Fred Kinney, along with Fred Kittinger, Roger Vinci, Jon Zorian, Bruce Behrens, and Mitch Paeglow with helping build the business. "In our early development, I received a lot of good financial advice and encouragement from my banker, Lynn Tucker," Laws adds.

In 1973, Laws purchased an old building at 1015 West Church Street that had been condemned and was part of an estate sale. "My offer of $40,000 was accepted and somehow my wife and I came up with the money, although all our friends thought we had lost our minds," he recalls. The building was later expanded and the fifteen-thousand-square-foot facility still serves as company headquarters.

In 1990, Laws sold the race engine building and speed shop portion of the business and retained the carburetor division, product development and machine shop portion, which became BLP Products, Inc.

The company that started with only five employees now employs 28 and generates annual sales in excess of $4 million. Laws' son, Mike, now serves as general manager and his daughter, Carol Richardson, is in charge of marketing and human resources.

For more information about BLP Products, visit www.blp.com on the Internet.

FLORIDA'S BLOOD CENTER, INC.

Florida's Blood Centers, Inc. (FBC) began in 1942 in a four-room facility at Orange General Hospital. Then known as the Central Florida Blood Bank, the center supplied blood for an average of one hundred transfusions a month. It was also the first transfusion service to provide stored blood in a Florida hospital.

The idea for Florida's Blood Centers came about when a group of physicians and local community leaders in Orlando saw the need for a centralized collection and distribution center for blood. When it was chartered, FBC became the first blood center in Florida and one of the first in the nation.

FBC is now the supplier of blood and blood products to seventy healthcare facilities in 21 counties, and provides more than 350,000 pints of blood each year, making it one of the largest independent blood banks in the nation.

FBC was among the first blood banks in the U.S. to establish a network for exchanging blood throughout the country. During the Gulf War, it was the second largest civilian supplier of blood to augment the military's supply. When terrorists attacked on September 11, 2001, it was the first blood bank to respond—within fifteen minutes. Four hundred units of blood were sent to the victims in New York City and the Washington, D.C. area.

Along with other blood centers in Food and Drug Administration (FDA). Because blood components are a special type of pharmaceutical production calledbiologics, the FDA licenses blood banks to manufacture and ship them across state lines. Florida's Blood Centers are inspected by the FDA for compliance with its Good Manufacturing Practices; the FDA also provides guidelines that must be followed in order for FBC to operate as a blood bank.

FBC is also a registration site for the National Marrow Donor Program. Through this program, potential donors or bone marrow and stem cells are found for those patients who have no genetically matched family member. For thousands of adults and children each year, this procedure may be their only chance for survival.

The story of Florida's Blood Centers is one of helping people. The blood bank has grown into a complex and sophisticated, multi-county operation with multiple branch locations and dozens of mobile units.

For more information about Florida's Blood Centers, call 1-800-DONATE or visit the website at www.floridasbloodcenters.org.

Above: The Blood Lab at Orlando General Hospital in 1942.

Below: A blood drive in the mid-1940s. Then the phlebotomists wore nurse uniforms.

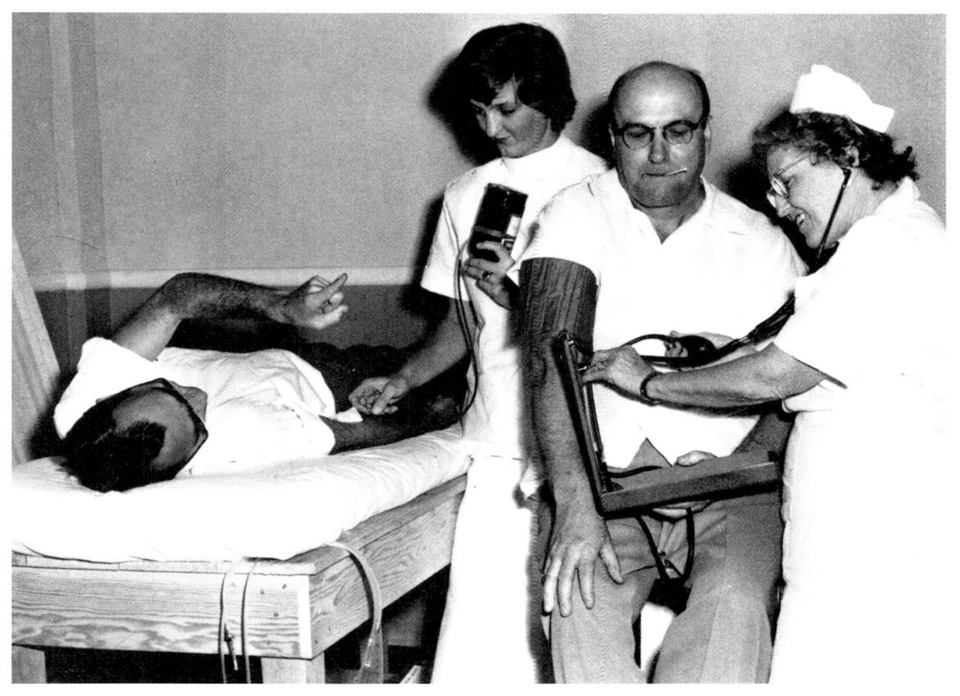

Crane Rental Corporation

Crane Rental Corporation has played a major role in the growth and development of Central Florida for nearly a half-century.

In its hometown of Orlando, for example, Crane Rental provided equipment and expertise that enabled prominent national contractors to create magnificent cityscapes, theme parks, hotels, industrial plants, and transportation infrastructure for what has become one of the nation's fastest growing cities, and the world's most popular travel destination.

Only a few miles away, at Cape Canaveral's Kennedy Space Center, Crane Rental equipment has been used to build, maintain, and enhance the facilities from which America's journeys into space have begun—from the earliest launch pads to the iconic Vehicle Assembly Building and the Space Shuttle Launch Tower.

Pete Ashlock founded Crane & Equipment Rental in 1960 with a loan from his father-in-law, Ephraim A. West. The company started business with three employees, one dragline, and one crane.

Over the years, Crane Rental has grown into a nationally recognized expert in heavy haul and rigging projects, serving its customers with more than 200 pieces of equipment, including 15-to-550-ton hydraulic cranes, crawler cranes up to 825 tons, tower cranes, and gantries.

Safety is always a top priority at Crane Rental and the company's strong safety program, which requires participation from all operators, drivers, service personnel, and other employees, was the winner of the Safety Improvement Program from the Specialized Carriers & Rigging Association (SC&RA).

The company was also the recipient of SC&RA's 2007 "Hauling Job of the Year" Award for moving 28 massive sugar production vessels—some weighing up to 137 tons—via barge across Lake Okeechobee to the new United States Sugar Corporation Plant in Clewiston, Florida.

Commercial and industrial contractors from across the U.S. and the Caribbean have come to depend on Crane Rigging for cost-effective rigging and hauling solutions for an ever-expanding portfolio of products, including servicing power plants, industrial, chemical, and refining facilities, colleges and convention centers, and major infrastructure construction projects such as Boston's "Big Dig" highway/tunnel project.

Even with this remarkable growth, Crane Rental Corporation retains the same values of a family-owned company that validates West's confidence in his son-in-law. Alan Ashlock, Pete's son and a twenty-four year company veteran, has served as president since 1988. Other key leaders include Martha Kirby, vice president of S/T; Barbara Ashlock Boyd, vice president for marketing and advertising; and Sean Spence, vice president of sales.

However, the true credit for Crane Rental Corporation's success goes to the nearly one hundred employees who each help fulfill the company's motto: "We Sell Nothing But Service."

A-1 Block Corporation

A-1 Block Corporation of Orlando, organized in 1952, has grown to become the leading producer of specialty concrete masonry units in the Southeast.

The family-owned firm, now in its third generation, was established by Anthony "Red" DaCato, who relocated to Orlando in 1952 to make concrete guard rails for the Florida Department of Transportation. After a short while, Red realized that Orlando needed concrete block, a trade he had learned back home in Connecticut. With the help of his wife, Ida, and financing from a previous employer and a machine manufacturer, A-1 Block Corporation began business with one machine and two laborers. Because they had no office at the time, Ida kept the books from the passenger seat of her car.

Ask anyone in the concrete industry about Red DaCato and they will tell you he was the hardest working man they ever met. Red manufactured blocks three days a week and delivered on the other three, resting only on Sunday. These were the days before forklifts, when each block had to be loaded and unloaded by hand. Although Red only had one arm, it was well known that he could work circles around anyone without a disability. Every obstacle he encountered was considered a mere 'speed bump' in his pursuit for success.

As the business grew, production was stepped up to six days a week and full-time delivery drivers were added to thestaff. Efficient machines were added to manufacture blocks more rapidly. By 1960 production was up to around five thousand units per day.

The 1970s brought another increase in production with the addition of even newer machines. When Disney came to Orlando, A-1 was ready to meet the demand. In the late 1970s, there was a big demand for architectural split face color units and these items were added to A-1's product line.

Red and Ida worked hard and by the early 1980s, A-1 Block had become the largest independent producer of concrete blocks in the Southeast.

The early 1990s saw the increasing popularity of ground face block and A-1 was there to meet the demand.

Today, A-1 Block Corporation runs seven block machines with a single-shift production of one hundred thousand units per day. The company operates manufacturing facilities in Orlando and Sanford and a distribution terminal in Lake Wales. A-1 Block has also branched out into the trucking industry, providing its own aggregate to all of their plants with Freeman Bros. LLC. Most recently in 2008, A-1 Concrete was formed to deliver pump mix to job sites with volumetric mixer trucks. A-1 Block is expanding its product line and services to meet the demand of its customers as demand is constantly changing.

A-1 Block attributes its success to its product line, hard-working employees, and service driven business which has created a large and loyal customer base. The company's extensive inventory and the ability to produce a wide range of products have made A-1 a dealer's supplier throughout the state.

A-1 Block Corporation is located at 1617 South Division Avenue in Orlando and on the Internet at www.a1block.com.

Below: A-1 Block's storage yard, 1960 (left). A-1 Block's newest facility, 2008 (right).

Bottom: In 1956 the original plant produced over a thousand blocks per day (left). In 2008, A-1 Block's newest production facility produces thirty-four thousand blocks per day (right).

Foote Steel Corporation

Foote Steel Corporation has been Central Florida's best source for quality structural steel components, fabrication, and installation at a fair price. The customer base consists of general contractors throughout the state of Florida. Quality and service are paramount in every job, regardless of size, scope or complexity.

Foote Steel projects have included such well-known landmarks as the Orlando Science Center, Daytona Ocean Center Expansion, and Coconut Point in Fort Myers. Other important projects include International Design Center in Estero, Arnold Palmer Hospital in Orlando, Hummer of Orlando, and St. Isaac Jogues Catholic Church in Orlando.

Foote Steel is a member of the American Institute of Steel Construction (AISC) and is certified to the AISC Standard for Steel Building Structures. AISC Certification sets a standard for the steel industry. Companies that are AISC Certified have been through a rigorous initial evaluation and are subject to yearly reviews. Quality Management Company, an independent auditing company, confirms that companies have the personnel, knowledge, organization, equipment, experience, capability, procedures, and commitment to produce the required quality of work. Foote Steel is the only company in the United States to achieve a perfect score with no corrective actions on annual audits performed thru 2007, including the initial audit in 2004.

The company was founded by George E. Foote, Sr., in 1950. George, Sr., started welding in shipyards during World War II and returned to Central Florida with the idea of opening a fabrication shop. He was joined in June 1965 by his son, George E. Foote, Jr. George, Sr., who retired in 2004, fostered a hands-on attitude with the fabrication of all products sent through the shop yard. George, Jr., began in the paint department, cleaning and painting steel, working his way through every facet of the business and is current owner/president.

Above: George E. Foote, Sr., with his wife, Phyllis Foote.

Below: Fabrication Plant, 1970.

The Foote family believes that personal relationships and trust are instrumental to building a successful business. Customers and employees alike can feel the friendliness, warmth, and loyalty that permeate the organization.

The business, which began on Colonial Drive, relocated in 1955 to 6635 Edgewater Drive in Orlando to take advantage of a Central Florida Railroad spur. This spur allowed direct delivery of materials from steel mills. Foote Steel has earned a reputation as a small shop that makes big things happen.

Foote Steel has the capability to fabricate commercial and residential structural steel products with unsurpassed quality. The fabrication shop houses several cranes including a ten-ton overhead crane; a saw with a capacity to cut forty-two by twenty-six inch beams, a state-of-the-art fully computerized five-axis beam line, and a five-hundred-ton cambering machine. Quality starts at project bid to final erection, which requires a one-hundred-percent inspection of all materials.

Currently, Foote Steel employs thirty-four skilled shop workers and thirty office personnel, including a full-service, in-house drafting department. All employees are dedicated to providing quality products and services at a reasonable cost.

For more information about Foote Steel Corporation, please visit www.footesteel.com.

Rollins College

In 1885, five Central Florida communities competed to become the site of a new college to be built under the auspices of the Florida Congregational Association. Chicago businessman Alonzo Rollins offered $100,000 if the school were built in the small town of Winter Park. Named in his honor, Rollins College opened its doors on the shores of Winter Park's beautiful Lake Virginia in November 1885.

The Rollins College campus began to take shape in the early twentieth century, when residence halls were built according to a "cottage plan" around the campus' centerpiece horseshoe drive. The coeducational college gained national visibility and financial security under the presidency of Hamilton Holt (1925-1949), who left a legacy including a distinguished tradition of experimental liberal arts education and the innovative Conference Plan, whereby students and professors shared learning around conference tables instead of in a traditional classroom setup. Aspects of this program continue at Rollins to this day and the College currently boasts an extraordinary student-to-faculty ratio of 10:1.

Consistently ranked by *U.S. News & World Report* as one of "America's Best Colleges," Rollins remains the oldest recognized college in Florida and continues to build on its tradition of academic excellence and innovation. With a student body of approximately thirty-five hundred, Rollins offers an undergraduate liberal arts degree, undergraduate and graduate evening studies degree programs at the Hamilton Holt School, and several full-time and part-time MBA options at the Crummer Graduate School of Business, which is consistently ranked among the nation's top business schools by *Forbes Magazine*.

Rollins offers twenty-three varsity sports and has received wide recognition for its successful Division II athletics program. A center for the arts in Central Florida, the College features the nationally recognized Cornell Fine Arts Museum, the historic Annie Russell Theatre, a popular music program, and the Winter With the Writers visiting authors series.

Under the leadership of former president Rita Bornstein (1990-2004), Rollins successfully completed the largest fundraising initiative in the College's history. Widely considered to have transformed the College and significantly strengthened its financial health, The Campaign For Rollins secured $160.2 million, providing support for academic programs, scholarships, faculty chairs, and facilities.

In April 2004, Lewis M. Duncan, former dean of Dartmouth College's Thayer School of Engineering, was elected as the fourteenth president of Rollins College. Under his leadership, in March 2007 Rollins hosted the "Rollins College Colloquy: Liberal Education and Social Responsibility in a Global Community." A continuation of the College's tradition of curricular exploration, the Colloquy convened thought leaders, including Maya Angelou, Francis Fukuyama, and Salman Rushdie, for a community conversation to consider the role of liberal education in the twenty-first century.

For more information about Rollins College, visit www.rollins.edu on the Internet.

Pineloch Management Corporation

The story of Southern Fruit Distributors and Pineloch Management Corporation began on April 28, 1902, when twelve-year-old Philip Caruso arrived in the United States from Sicily. Starting as a produce vendor in New York, by 1924 Philip had the largest single produce wholesale company of fruits and vegetables in the country.

In 1925, he moved to Florida and began purchasing fruit and shipping it to his companies' New York branches. In 1926, Philip organized and incorporated Southern Fruit Distributors, Inc., purchased the patent and copyright of the Bluebird label, and opened his first fresh fruit packing house in Lisbon, Lake County, Florida, to buy and pack citrus for New York distributors. Other packing houses in Alturas and Winter Garden were added, as well as a small canning plant. By 1940 space was limited in Winter Garden and the processing plant was moved to its present location in South Orlando. After World War II, Philip's sons and son-in-law joined business. By 1946, Austin was president (age thirty-two, chief administrative officer, supervising production, sales and administration), Joseph was vice president (age thirty-one, grove operations including cultivation and harvesting, supervising truck and garage operations), John Walsh was vice president (age thirty-three, supervising plant maintenance, repairs, new construction and canning plant production) and Philip Peter was secretary and treasurer (age twenty-seven, supervising warehouse shipping operations and sales and warehouse stocks in the Southeastern U.S.).

Philip died 1963 at the age of seventy-two. In 1987, he was inducted into the Mid-Florida Business Hall of Fame.

By 1986, Southern Fruit reported $95 million in sales and was ranked fifth on the "Golden 50 of Central Florida", a listing of the top firms in the area. The citrus industry began changing with global competition, freezes, environmental issues, and urbanization. The plant site was now in downtown Orlando. A decision to sell was made by the Caruso family, and on its sixtieth anniversary in 1987, Southern Fruit sold its rights to the Bluebird label and its marketing operations to Citrus World of Lake Wales, processors of Florida's Natural brand juice.

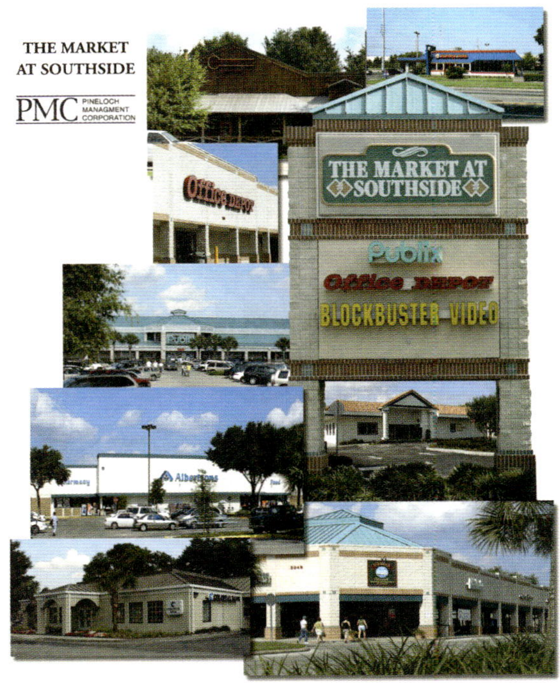

With the remaining assets, the third generation helped change the landscape in South Orlando. Pineloch Management Corporation was incorporated in 1987 and three Caruso family members provide the current management team: President Jim Caruso, Vice President Phylis Caruso, and Facilities Director Paul Caruso. Other family members help guide the business through the board of directors.

Today Pineloch is a diversified leader involved in real estate leasing, management, warehousing and agriculture, including top-tier diversified properties throughout Central Florida such as The Market at Southside (retail), Southgate Commerce Center and Pineloch Business Park (commercial/office), and Pineloch Industrial Park (industrial) in Winter Garden.

For more information about Pineloch Management Corporation and Southern Warehousing, please visit www.pineloch.com and www.southernwarehouse.com.

FINFROCK® DESIGN-MANUFACTURE-CONSTRUCT

Finfrock®, headquartered in Orlando, is the largest designer, manufacturer and constructor of parking structures in the United States. As a design-builder and manufacturer of buildings utilizing precast concrete, Finfrock's ability to standardize the building components and economically integrate other building subsystems is unique to the construction industry.

Finfrock was founded in 1945 by Robert J. D. Finfrock, who had been the Florida representative for the Portland Cement Association. Realizing the need for precast and prestressed concrete to meet the building boom that followed World War II, Finfrock began with a small company located in downtown Orlando. The company moved to its present location at 2400 Apopka Boulevard in 1951. Finfrock's son, Robert, joined the company in 1965 and now serves as president.

The dramatic growth of Finfrock began in the mid-1990s with the transformation from a manufacturer of concrete products to a design-manufacturer-construct business. "That's what really spurred our growth," explains Robert Finfrock. "We didn't feel our products were being used in an efficient manner by the construction industry and we needed to take a larger role in the actual design and construction."

Finfrock's unique, turnkey project delivery system ensures early and accurate pricing, reduced risk, improved quality, lower costs, and improved bottom line performance for its clients.

A vertically integrated firm, Finfrock provides all the services necessary for construction from design, through manufacturing and the actual construction.

"The unique nature of our business is that we sell a product—a completed building—instead of a series of services like most design-build firms," explains Finfrock. "Our goal is to deliver value to our customers."

Finfrock has grown to nearly four hundred employees since its transformation to a design-manufacturer-construct business and a third generation of the Finfrock family is now active in the firm. Allen Finfrock is vice president of design, Bill Finfrock is vice president of sales, and Dan Finfrock serves as vice president of manufacturing.

For more information about Finfrock, please visit www.finfrockdmc.com.

Above: Rollins College parking structure, Winter Park, Florida.

Below: Offices at Veranda Park, Orlando Florida.

Orange County Regional History Center

The Orange County Regional History Center first opened in 1942 as the Historical Museum housed in the 1892 red brick Orange County Courthouse at the corner of Central Boulevard and Magnolia Avenue. The original museum featured a pioneer kitchen exhibit created for the Central Florida Centennial Celebration. The popular exhibit remained open after the centennial, and, through public donations of historical objects including books, papers, and photographs, grew to fill two rooms in the old courthouse.

From 1957 until 1963, the collection was in storage while the county built an addition to the 1927 Orange County Courthouse on the site of the demolished 1892 courthouse. The museum reopened in the Courthouse Annex in 1963 under the auspices of the Orange County Historical Commission, a new county department established by the County Commissioners in 1957 to ensure fiscal and legal stability. By 1970 the county government needed the space in the annex, so the museum collection was moved again to the second floor of the Christ Building, formerly the Elks Club, a few doors away on Central Boulevard.

The Orange County Historical Society, Inc., organized in 1971 to raise money for a permanent museum building, opened the Historical Museum in Loch Haven Park in 1976. In 2000 the museum moved again, back to where it had started at Central Boulevard and Magnolia Avenue. The vacated 1927 Courthouse was restored to become the Orange County Regional History Center, and the Orange County Historical Society became the Historical Society of Central Florida, Inc., operating the History Center in partnership with the Orange County Board of County Commissioners.

In 2006 the Orange County Regional History Center was awarded accreditation by the American Association of Museums, the highest honor a museum can receive. The history museum also was accepted as an affiliate of the Smithsonian Institution that same year. Its program recognizes select organizations for having goals compatible with the Smithsonian's mission, who maintain the high standard of excellence that is synonymous with Smithsonian's exhibition presentation and museum education.

Today, the Orange County Regional History Center continues to showcase the vast collections of the Historical Society of Central Florida, Inc. The History Center features three floors of permanent exhibitions that take visitors on a journey through the region's fascinating transition from Indian settlement to small town surrounded by citrus groves and cattle ranches to today's tourist-centric community. The museum also presents nationally important, limited-run exhibitions, bringing unique aspects of history to the Central Florida community.

Epoch Properties, Inc.

Epoch Properties, Inc., founded in 1970, has built and managed rental apartment communities across the nation from California to Florida.

"The company began when founding partner Earl Downs hired John McClintock and me and gave us the opportunity to run the company," explains James H. "Jim" Pugh, Jr., chairman. "Other than the founder, none of us were older than thirty years old in the early days, so we went out and started doing joint ventures with life insurance companies. We didn't know you were supposed to be older to do what we were doing."

In the mid-1970s, soon after the company was organized, there was a significant recession in the housing industry and developing multifamily apartments became next to impossible in the Southeast. To keep the company going, the partners relocated development operations to Texas for four years.

Epoch Properties has now developed more than 31,500 multifamily living units, with a value in excess of $2 billion. Epoch Management, Inc., formed in 1975 to manage the properties, currently manages nearly nine thousand units.

Although Epoch's focus is on the southeastern U.S., particularly Florida, Texas and the Carolinas, the company has developed as far north as Virginia and as far west as California.

Among Epoch's recent projects are Cumberland Park in Orlando, the Lofts at Uptown Altamonte in Altamonte Springs, Las Ventanas in Boynton Beach, and Las Brisas in Austin, Texas.

In addition to Downs, McClintock and Pugh, other key leaders in the company's early days were Gerry Ogier, Tom Bohannon, Wally Temple, Jim Pitts, Bob Vergnolle, Jack Sharp, Bob Bentel and John Ariko.

Currently, Pugh serves as chairman of the company, Kyle Riva is president of Epoch Properties, and Greg Jacoby is president of Epoch Management.

"Jim Pugh has always been very actively involved with civic and philanthropic endeavors," says Riva. "Giving back is very important to Jim."

Pugh, a graduate of the University of Florida, serves as chairman of the Dr. P. Phillips Orlando Performing Arts Center Board, is a past president of the Orlando Utilities Commission, past member of the Greater Orlando Aviation Authority, former chairman of the Orlando-Orange County Expressway Authority, and former chairman of the Board of Trustees of the Atlantic Center for the Arts.

Pugh was named one of "the most influential Floridians" by Florida Trend magazine, and one of the "most influential businessmen" by Orlando Business Journal.

Epoch Properties and Epoch Management have a combined employment of over two hundred persons and is headquartered in Winter Park. The firm maintains other offices in Boynton Beach, Florida and Austin, Texas.

Below: The Lofts at Uptown Altamonte Luxury Apartments, Altamont Springs, Florida.

Bottom: Villa Toscana at Lakes of Laguna Luxury Apartment Homes, West Palm Beach, Florida.

Cuthill & Eddy, LLC

Cuthill & Eddy LLC, was founded in 1975 by Certified Public Accountants Carson L. Eddy and R.W. "Bill" Cuthill. The two had one major goal; to organize a firm that would grow and prosper but at the same time allow them to work only thirty-five hours per week. They were very much interested in spending more time with their families and in service to their community.

The firm opened for business in a vacant office loaned to them by another small accounting firm. The office had only one desk and since Bill was the managing partner he got the side with knee space. After a few months, the office was moved to the fifth floor of the Southland Building at the corner of Lee and Wymore Roads.

Bill and Carson decided to concentrate on audit clients, feeling that their main strength was in that area. The two turned down many small bookkeeping and write-up engagements to focus on providing quality service to their audit clients, a strategy that allowed them to provide a wide range of superior audit, tax and management consulting services to many of Central Florida's most respected organizations.

The firm hired its first professional associate in 1977 and, by 1979, their were four professionals backed by a support person. One of the first professionals hired was Vic Incinelli, who later became a partner. By 1982 a tax partner was added and the firm had grown to ten professionals and two support staff. The construction of their office building at 1941 Lee Road was completed and moved into.

The period from 1983 through 1996 was challenging, but productive. The firm lost two partners during that period, including the tax partner, and changed managing partners. To offset the loss of the tax partner, the firm hired another tax specialist and merged with a small tax practitioner. The building on Lee Road was sold in 1997 and the firm moved into its current location in the BankFirst Building on Morse Boulevard in Winter Park.

It was also during this period that Cuthill & Eddy acquired a litigation practice and began what is now Quantum Consulting Group LLC, a Certified Public Accounting Firm providing litigation support and forensic accounting services to law firms throughout Central Florida.

Bill retired as partner in 2001. Subsequently, Todd Hitchins (tax, 2003) and Jennifer Christensen (audit, 2006) became partners in the firm.

In an effort to continue providing quality and excellence in the ever changing world of public accounting, the partners of Cuthill & Eddy were acquired in October of 2007 and made equity partners in the firm of Carr Riggs & Ingram LLC (CRI), based in Enterprise, Alabama. CRI is the eighth largest Certified Public Accounting Firm in the Southeast and the thirty-sixth largest in the nation.

In the end, the founder's goal has been met; the professionals continue to work thirty-five hours per week and have time to devote to family and contribute to the community.

Carr, Riggs & Ingram is located at 1031 West Morse Boulevard, Suite 200 in Winter Park, Florida and on the Internet at www.cricpa.com.

Above: Carson L. Eddy.

Below: From left to right, Vic Incinelli, Bill Carr, Carson Eddy, Jennifer Christensen and Todd Hitchins.

FERRAN SERVICES & CONTRACTING, INC.

Integrity, service, quality.... these are the common threads that weave several companies together to create the fabric that is Ferran Services & Contracting Inc. of Orlando, Florida. The group had its beginnings in 1967 when Harry A. Ferran, an Orlando native and fifth generation Floridian, purchased Ward Air Conditioning. He acquired the company from Taylor D. Ward, the former director of advertising for Kimberly-Clark Corporation. The company previously known as H.A. Daugherty was purchased and renamed by Ward in June of 1952. Its distinctive dark green uniforms remain a Ferran trademark today.

In 1981, Harry purchased Johnson Electric, merging it with Ward Air Conditioning and thus creating Ferran Engineering Group Inc. Johnson Electric was originally founded in 1913 by A.B. Johnson. He began the company's operations from his home, carrying a roll of wire over each handlebar of his bicycle and his hand tools on his back. The 1921, Orlando City Directory lists what is probably the first Johnson Electric location at 11 Court Street. Johnson's reputation as an excellent electrician and honest businessman helped the company grow from one bicycle riding electrician to a fleet of trucks.

Harry's goal was to make Ferran Engineering Group the definitive choice for service and installation in Central Florida so, in 1982; Harry created Avery Plumbing. Harry extended his operation to Volusia County by purchasing D.W. Browning Plumbing & Air Conditioning in 1986. Ferran's slogan said it all: "The Best Service Companies in Orlando Have One Name; Ferran Engineering Group."

After Harry's death in 1993, his son Robert C. Ferran took over the business. Rob added several benefits to the employee package and hired Adolph "Dolph" Marmetschke to run its operations. The company continued to prosper and grow.

After running the company for seven years, Dolph purchased Ferran Services & Contracting in 2000. Under Dolph's leadership, Ferran was able to maintain its headquarters at 530 Grand Street while its two original buildings were demolished in 2006. Final construction of the new Ferran building was completed in April 2007. The new building's unique design is a representation of all the Ferran Divisions; Air Conditioning, Electrical, and Plumbing and is quickly becoming a landmark in the downtown area. Dolph's commitment to quality workmanship and ethical business practices has ensured the success and continued growth of Ferran Services & Contracting well into the future.

Above: Johnson Electric management and employees gather in front of their headquarters at 119 East Pine Street, downtown Orlando in 1926. Founder A.B. Johnson (with straw hat) is standing third from right.

Below: Ferran Services & Contracting's new headquarters located at 530 Grand Street in downtown Orlando.

First American Title Insurance Company

Since the horse and buggy era, First American Title Insurance Company has been serving the Central Florida real estate market and community. It just may be the oldest company in Central Florida with more than 125 years of service.

Originally known as Fidelity Title and Guaranty Company, its first office stood on the southwest corner of Court and Oak (now Wall) Street in downtown Orlando. The company grew by acquiring the Abstract Corporation of Deland and Lake Abstract in Lake County. Acquisitions such as these, enabled it to expand its operations beyond Orange County.

The company was founded by D. S. Shine and Colonel J. N. Bradshaw, but was acquired, soon after, by William Beardall, Sr., and remained in the hands of the Beardall family for three generations. In 1985 the company was purchased by R. Harris Turner, Larry P. Deal, and Carl Bauchle. It became part of the First American Title Insurance family in 1994. Larry and Carl remain with the company to this day.

Although its name and location have changed throughout the years, its continued commitment to quality, efficiency, and personal service has not.

Today, First American Title operates a network of offices and agents throughout the world and is a leader in title technology. A Fortune 375 company, First American is the largest title insurance company in the United States.

Committed to the concept of local service and support, First American continues to serve the residential and commercial real estate market in Central Florida by being a leader in title automation, facilities, and closing services. With offices in Orlando, Lake Mary, Winter Park, Altamonte Springs, Mount Dora, and Deland, as well as a network of agents throughout Central Florida, the company is one of the largest title insurance firms in the Orlando area. Despite tremendous growth, service remains personalized and customer focused.

First American strives to be more than just a title company, and is committed to serve all the needs of real estate professionals and attorneys in Central Florida with a wide range of quality services.

From its early days, community involvement has always been important to First American. Organizations such as the Central Florida Blood Bank, American Heart Association, Habitat for Humanity, United Way of Central Florida, and the local PBS station all benefit from hours of community service and contributions by its employees.

After more than 125 years, First American continues to work diligently to serve the real estate industry and to be a leader in automation and technology without losing its commitment to local services.

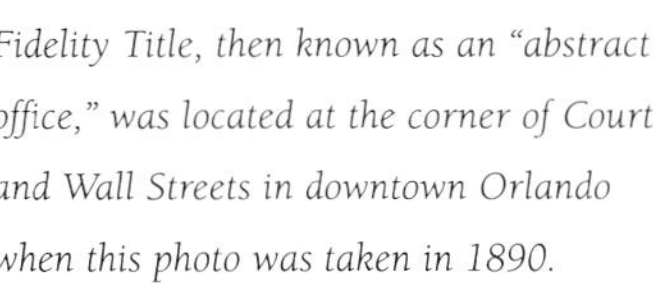

Fidelity Title, then known as an "abstract office," was located at the corner of Court and Wall Streets in downtown Orlando when this photo was taken in 1890.

Dora Landscaping Company

From its beginnings as a small lawn mowing service in 1976, Dora Landscaping has grown to become the forty-fifth largest landscape contractor in the nation. The family-owned business is responsible for the creation and maintenance of such award winning installations as Disney's All Star Resort, Animal Kingdom Observatory, Chase Manhattan Plaza, and Sea World Aquatica.

With a highly trained staff of nearly one hundred employees, Dora Landscaping is known for the quality of its premium plant materials and the beauty and curb appeal of both its residential and commercial projects. Dora's top superintendents have more than seventy-five years combined experience and its fleet of up-to-date equipment is managed so no 'down-time' is experienced.

Operated by founder Jim Oyler, his wife, Lisa, and General Manager Jamie Beaulieu, Dora Landscaping strives for excellence by providing only the highest quality service and workmanship at reasonable cost.

Dora Landscaping operates three divisions—landscape construction, professional grounds maintenance, and irrigation—in addition to an on-site thirty-acre nursery, Southern Landscape Growers.

The Landscape Construction Division provides highly qualified and trained superintendents to manage each project. A Florida certified landscape contractor is on staff and the operations managers have decades of experience in managing beautiful and environmentally friendly landscape installations. With its large fleet of trucks and the latest equipment, Dora is prepared to tackle any project, regardless of size. Best of all, Dora takes pride in bringing in projects on time and within budget.

Dora's Professional Grounds Maintenance Division provides comprehensive grounds management services, including basic ground management, Integrated Pest Management (IPM), fertilization, arbor care and floriculture. Dora's staff includes trained certified pest control operators (CPO) licensed by the State of Florida to apply pest control products. A licensed Arborist is also on staff.

The Irrigation Division provides "build-to-suit" and "design-build" irrigation systems to meet any customer's need. Dora's irrigation superintendents are trained by Rainbird to install, maintain, and manage Maxi-Com Irrigation Systems. In addition, Dora is certified by the State of Florida to pull permits.

Dora Landscaping's wholesale nursery, Southern Landscape Growers, occupies a large portion of the company's thirty-plus-acre facility in Apopka. Specializing in woody ornamentals and container grown trees, Southern Landscape is able to "grow out" various materials for future projects. This allows the company to meet and exceed the expectations of the landscape designer. In addition to retail operations, Southern Landscape Growers provides premium materials for retrofit grounds maintenance projects.

Dora Landscaping is located at 4301 Hogshead Road in Apopka. For additional information on Dora Landscaping and the projects they have completed, please visit www.doralandscape.com.

Control Specialists Company

Control Specialists Company, a traffic engineering firm, provides a full range of services including design-build and system installation projects, traffic systems and equipment sales, and technical services, backed by twenty-four hour, seven days a week maintenance and technical support.

Control Specialists was founded in Orlando in 1965 by Arthur W. Belden, Jr. as a sales company specializing in traffic engineering controls. Since 1970 the firm has provided outstanding contract service and maintenance for traffic signal systems control for both private and municipal organizations. The company manages and maintains more than five hundred locations for emergency repair service, providing twenty-four hour "on-call" response, seven days a week. Because the company is capable of performing any task, it continues to save its customers significant amounts of money each year with planned monthly proactive and preventative maintenance.

Arthur Belden served as an officer in the U.S. Navy and received a B.S. degree in Electrical Engineering from the University of Louisville's Speed School of Engineering in 1947. He came to Florida in 1949 when he was chosen as one of the first fifty employees of the Joint Long Range Proving Ground facility at Patrick Air Force Base, later known as NASA. Belden joined Ward Engineering Company as a manufacturer's representative in 1956 and became the company president in 1963.

Belden and his wife, Alice, founded Control Specialists Company in the Florida room of their Orlando home. The two established a solid foundation and, leaning on their faith and trust in God, built the business, which continues to grow and flourish. Belden's father, Colonel A.W. Belden, set up an accounting system for the company and served as treasurer for many years.

Above: Founder Art Belden with O'Donoghue family during visit by Governor Jeb Bush.

Below: Downtown Winter Park is one of the many locations served by Control Specialists.

Control Specialists began their efforts in traffic signal installation and maintenance in 1973, using a pick-up truck with an adjustable ladder. The company's first Florida DOT construction project was as a subcontractor to Hubbard Construction in 1974.

W. Bruce O'Donoghue, the Belden's son, joined the company full time in 1977 after receiving his degree in Urban Studies from the University of Florida where he was inducted into University's Hall of Fame. Having worked as the company janitor in high school, O'Donoghue served the company in various capacities. In 1990, when Belden retired as president and CEO, O'Donoghue took over the reins. Alice, served as company secretary for many years and continues to serve on the corporation's Board of Directors.

Control Specialists employs fifty people at its headquarters in Winter Park and in their office in Atlanta. The company has received numerous awards for its performance and service, including the Florida Department of Transportation's "I MADE A DIFFERENCE" Award and the InterTraffic's "Innovation Award".

Belden's business philosophy has always been to "serve the customer first." This philosophy has proven successful, providing for long-standing customer relations. Every employee, regardless of position, demonstrates this philosophy in their daily work.

For more information about Control Specialists Company and its services, please visit www.controlspecialists.com.

Walt Disney World

As early as 1958, Walt Disney began thinking about building an East Coast complement to the hugely successful Disneyland® Park in California. To find just the right location, he started sending studio executives across the country in secrecy, where they checked into hotels under assumed names and made anonymous inquiries about available land. They worried that if they were identified, or if Walt Disney was spotted, the project would garner unwanted attention and land prices would soar.

After considering several cities on the East Coast, a research study was commissioned to determine the best location for Walt's expansion plans. Florida was the chosen spot. Several places in Central Florida were considered, including areas near Ocala and Deland, but the team eventually settled on the Orlando area for its proximity to the intersection of Florida's Turnpike and the new Interstate 4. Land was purchased secretly piece by piece and, in the end, the company paid just more than $5 million for about 27,000 acres straddling both Orange and Osceola Counties.

Rumors began to circulate regarding who was buying up the large parcels of land, with names like Ford, McDonnell-Douglas and Howard Hughes mentioned as possibilities. But after the *Orlando Sentinel* ran a front-page article proclaiming its certainty that it was Disney, company officials decided to make an announcement. On November 15, 1965, Walt Disney held a news conference with Roy Disney and Florida Governor Haydon Burns at the Cherry Plaza Hotel on Central Avenue in downtown Orlando. The exact plans for the Florida project were still uncertain, but Walt Disney described his ideas about a city of the future, along with a vacation retreat including parks, resort hotels and golf courses.

Unfortunately, Walt Disney passed away before any construction took place, but his team of Imagineers was determined to continue without him. Roy Disney postponed retirement to personally oversee the completion of the project, and it was his decision to name the overall resort Walt Disney World as a tribute to his brother.

The site's first theme park, Magic Kingdom® Park, opened October 1, 1971. Today, the Walt Disney World Resort is a forty square-mile, world-class entertainment and recreation center featuring four theme parks (Magic Kingdom® Park, Epcot®, Disney's Hollywood Studios™ and Disney's Animal Kingdom® Theme Park); 2 water adventure parks, 23 resort hotels, 81 holes of golf on 5 courses; Disney's Wedding Pavilion; Disney's Wide World of Sports® Complex; and Downtown Disney, an entertainment-shopping-dining complex.

For more information about Walt Disney World Resort, visit the website at www.waltdisneyworld.com.

Above: Cinderella Castle in the Magic Kingdom® Park at Walt Disney World® Resort.

Below: Cinderella Castle under construction at the Magic Kingdom® Park at Walt Disney World® Resort.

LYNX

LYNX, the public transportation service for Orange, Seminole, and Osceola Counties, began in 1931 as the Orlando Transit Company. The company, founded by Sidney Swope, Sr., offered four routes to serve the city of Orlando and one route to serve Winter Park. There was no bus station in the early days, so buses simply lined up along Main Street until departure time.

The system's first terminal was built between Pine and Central Streets in 1964 and, in 1971, Orlando Transit Company was granted a Gray Line Charter License. The Swope family turned its attention to the more lucrative Gray Line business and Orlando and Orange County were soon faced with the possibility of losing public transportation.

To insure the continuation of public transportation, Orange County signed an agreement with Seminole and Osceola Counties in 1972 to form the Orange-Seminole-Osceola Transportation Authority, better known as OSOTA. When Orlando Transit abandoned public transportation, seventeen employees and a fleet of twenty-three buses were acquired by OSOTA. Thirty-three air conditioned buses were added to the OSOTA fleet the following year.

OSOTA's name was changed to Tri County Transit in 1984 and, the following year, a new terminal was completed. The terminal received the "Gold Brick" award for its combination of visual appeal and function.

The 1990s were a period of tremendous growth and change for the transit system. A conscious effort was made to improve the image of public transportation in Orlando, an executive director was hired and a decision was made to change the name from Tri-County Transit. A public 'Whatchamacallit" contest was conducted and the winning name selected was LYNX. This became the official name under which the Central Florida Regional Transportation Authority provides service.

LYNX has broken ridership records twenty-four times in the past twenty-five years. In October 1993, LYNX carried one million riders in a single month for the first time, and the annual passenger total reached 11.1 million–a new record. In 2007, LYNX provided more than 26 million passenger trips.

LYNX's accomplishments were recognized in 1996 and 1998 when it received the "Outstanding Achievement in Public Transit" Award from the American Public Transit Association. This is one of the major awards presented for public transportation systems nationwide and confirmed LYNX's reputation as one of the country's premier systems.

The agency moved to its current location—LYNX Central Station—in 2004 and opened a new operations center in 2007. In addition, LYNX recently celebrated the tenth anniversary of LYMMO, the nation's first fully functional Bus Rapid Transit System.

Today, the LYNX service area stretches over 2,500 square miles, making it one of the largest transit systems in the nation.

For additional information on LYNX, including fees, routes and schedules, please visit www.golynx.com.

Alcorn McBride Inc.

If you have visited a major theme park anywhere in the world, it is likely you have come into contact with products from Alcorn McBride Inc.

Alcorn McBride is the leading manufacturer of show control, audio and video equipment for the theme park industry. Their equipment is also used in museums, restaurants, visitor centers, retail stores, kiosks, and trade shows around the world.

Alcorn McBride was founded in Southern California in 1986 by Steve Alcorn, an engineer who worked on Epcot and was Chief Operating Officer at Linn Electronics; an electronic musical instrument manufacturer.

As the company grew, Steve gradually brought in other engineers who had worked with him in the past. Most had Disney experience, and many had also worked in the electronic music industry. The company moved to Orlando in 1989, largely because he and the employees valued the more relaxed lifestyle and better environment.

Alcorn McBride initially occupied rented space in an industrial park, then, in 1992, purchased an office building in Metrowest at 3300 South Hiawassee Road. The firm also owns a warehouse near the airport. A subsidiary owns offices in France, near Paris Disneyland.

The Alcorn McBride staff has grown to nearly twenty engineers and support staff, and keeps another twenty contract manufacturing people busy, assembling and testing products.

The company's best selling Digital Video Machine is a hardback book-sized box that plays many hours of high quality video and audio with no moving parts. They also make the Digital Binloop, a multi-channel audio playback system used in nearly every theme park attraction.

Thousands of pieces of Alcorn McBride electronic equipment are installed in all of Central Florida's theme parks. Much of it has been operating, without a power cycle or reset, for a decade or more. Alcorn McBride recently provided the GPS-triggered audio players for the I-Ride Trolley and the GPS-triggered video players for the Mears-operated Disney's Magical Express.

Alcorn McBride has been named an *Inc.* 5000 Fastest Growing Company, and received the Florida Governor's Award for best new product for its high definition video player.

Looking to the future, Steve says his goal is to help his employees live up to Alcorn McBride's mission statement, which is simply, "Have fun, make money."

For product information, trade show locations, and much more you may visit Alcorn McBride on the Internet at www.alcorn.com.

Above: Alcorn McBride has been bringing you the sights and sounds behind the scenes in nearly all the world's theme parks for more than twenty years.

Below: Alcorn McBride's Orlando staff.

HUBBARD CONSTRUCTION COMPANY

Since 1920, Hubbard Construction Company of Orlando has literally paved the way for hundreds of public and private projects that have helped Florida develop and grow. Along with Blythe Construction, the Hubbard Group ranks as America's fourteenth largest domestic heavy construction company with combined annual revenues of $450 million.

Also included under the Hubbard umbrella are Orlando Paving Company, East Coast Paving, and Atlantic Coast Asphalt.

This huge enterprise began when Francis Evans Hubbard began hauling sand onto construction projects in Florence, South Carolina, using mules and wagons. The business prospered and Hubbard soon had twelve employees working for his hauling/construction business.

Hubbard moved to Florida in 1924 where his first jobs were clearing and grading in Lake County. At this time, Hubbard entered into a partnership with Joe McKown and created the firm Hubbard and McKown. This partnership was dissolved in 1927 and Hubbard ran the company by himself until 1928 when he partnered with James H. Craggs and T. E. Cleary to form Hubbard Construction Company.

Although many construction firms were forced out of business during the Great Depression, Hubbard Construction was able to borrow enough money to meet the payroll and continue operating. Because of this, the company grew stronger, even during the adverse business conditions during the depression.

In 1936, Hubbard and Langston Construction Company created a joint venture and by 1937, the company was doing $300,000 to $400,000 worth of business annually. That joint venture was dissolved in 1946.

Francis Evans Hubbard, who had become a noted philanthropist, died in 1954, leaving a large legacy for Orange Memorial Hospital, now Orange Regional Medical Center. The hospital dedicated a five-story hospital wing in his name.

The company continued to grow under the direction of Frank M. Hubbard, and the Orlando Paving Company was established in 1954 in conjunction with Jack Blythe.

Hubbard Construction received its first contract from Disney in 1967 and has been instrumental in work at Epcot and other Disney projects, including the Disney Monorail System.

The company was sold to Selby Sullivan in 1984 and, in 1988; Sullivan sold to Enterprise Jean-Lefebvre of Paris, France, which merged with Eurovia in 2000.

The scope of Hubbard's work today includes complex highway projects, site development, paving, utility and drainage systems, surveying, RAP and hot mix sales, and state-of-the-art bridge building.

Hubbard Construction, with more than twelve hundred employees, maintains its corporate office in Winter Park, with asphalt and construction offices in Orlando, West Palm, Tampa, and Jacksonville.

Apex Environmental Engineering & Compliance, Inc.

Above (from left to right): Senior Vice President Chris Parent, President and CEO Rod Vargas, and Vice President Dennis Theoret.

Apex Environmental Engineering & Compliance, Inc. (Apex Environmental) was established in 1997 when Chris Parent and Rod Vargas, P.E. decided to open an environmental consulting firm which could offer quality services while providing a work/home/personal life balance for all who worked there.

In only ten years, the firm grew from two employees and revenues of $75,000 to thirty-two employees and revenues of $7.4 million. In 2006, Apex Environmental earned a place on *Inc.* magazine's list of 500 fastest-growing privately held businesses in America.

Apex Environmental provides a wide range of environmental, health, safety, construction, and engineering consulting services. The firm's project teams include engineers, geologists, specialized consultants, and certified contractors to provide a full range of services.

Apex Environmental draws upon extensive industry knowledge, distinguished professionals and innovative technologies to develop solutions to complex environmental, engineering safety, and health issues.

During the firm's early days, Parent and Vargas did whatever was necessary to get the job done. If they were doing technical work, they appeared as technicians. Some clients never realized the workers digging holes and doing manual labor were actually engineers.

Apex Environmental's first employee was Michael Piland, a fireman at Station 1 in Orlando, who brought tremendous health and safety expertise and an incredible work ethic to his off-days job. The company continues to hire either ex-firemen or firemen on their off-days because of their incredible work ethic and experience.

In 2000, Dennis Theoret, P.G. became a partner in the firm, bringing his technical abilities as a geologist and experience managing large projects for the Department of Defense and private clients. Vargas serves as president and CEO of Apex Environmental, Parent is senior vice president, and Theoret is vice president. Vargas was named Florida's Small Business Person of the Year in 2007 for the State of Florida by the Small Business Administration (SBA).

The company's main office is located at 6824 Hanging Moss Road in Orlando. Other offices are located in Merritt Island and Tampa.

Since its beginning, Apex Environmental has contributed its experience, time and resources to those in need. Company employees have mentored local businesses and provided pro bono engineering and consulting work to help worthy causes.

"The environment at Apex Environmental continues to be low key and easy going, and we continue to be fortunate to have employees of value and fun to work with," says Vargas. "We have a great time both at work and during our time of relaxation as a group. We stress the need of all of us to have a balanced life where work does not hinder family or personal time."

Sponsors

About the Authors

TANA MOSIER PORTER

Tana Mosier Porter, PH.D., is a graduate of the University of Toledo, and author of two books and several articles on Toledo history and an article published in the *Florida Historical Quarterly* on Orlando's African American community.

CASSANDRA FYOTEK

Cassandra Fyotek completed undergraduate work in History at the University of Central Florida and is currently pursuing a Masters Degree in Public History. She was formerly the Collections Assistant at the Orange County Regional History Center.

STEPHANIE GAUB

Stephanie Gaub is the Collections Manager at the Orange County Regional History Center. She is originally from Titusville, Pennsylvania, and completed her Master's Degree in Historical Administration at Eastern Illinois University.

CYNTHIA CARDONA MELÉNDEZ

Cynthia Cardona Meléndez is the curator of collections at the Orange County Regional History Center. A native of St. Cloud, Florida, Cynthia earned both her B.A. and M.A. in History from the University of Central Florida.

GARRET KREMER-WRIGHT

Garret Kremer-Wright works as the Archivist at the Orange County Regional History Center. A native of Jefferson City, Missouri, he received his Master's in Public History from Wright State University.

BARBARA KNOWLES

Barbara Knowles is the Research Coordinator at the Orange County Regional History Center. She obtained a Bachelor's Degree in English from Bowling Green State University and a Master's Degree in Education from the University of Miami. She researches and writes exhibits for the museum and facilitates the traveling exhibit program.

For more information about the following publications or about publishing your own book, please call Historical Publishing Network at 800-749-9790 or visit www.lammertinc.com.

Black Gold: The Story of Texas Oil & Gas

Garland: A Contemporary History

Historic Abilene: An Illustrated History

Historic Albuquerque: An Illustrated History

Historic Amarillo: An Illustrated History

Historic Anchorage: An Illustrated History

Historic Austin: An Illustrated History

Historic Baldwin County: A Bicentennial History

Historic Baton Rouge: An Illustrated History

Historic Beaufort County: An Illustrated History

Historic Beaumont: An Illustrated History

Historic Bexar County: An Illustrated History

Historic Birmingham: An Illustrated History

Historic Brazoria County: An Illustrated History

Historic Charlotte:
An Illustrated History of Charlotte and Mecklenburg County

Historic Cheyenne: A History of the Magic City

Historic Comal County: An Illustrated History

Historic Corpus Christi: An Illustrated History

Historic DeKalb County: An Illustrated History

Historic Denton County: An Illustrated History

Historic Edmond: An Illustrated History

Historic El Paso: An Illustrated History

Historic Erie County: An Illustrated History

Historic Fairbanks: An Illustrated History

Historic Gainesville & Hall County: An Illustrated History

Historic Gregg County: An Illustrated History

Historic Hampton Roads: Where America Began

Historic Hancock County: An Illustrated History

Historic Henry County: An Illustrated History

Historic Houston: An Illustrated History

Historic Illinois: An Illustrated History

Historic Kern County:
An Illustrated History of Bakersfield and Kern County

Historic Lafayette:
An Illustrated History of Lafayette & Lafayette Parish

Historic Laredo:
An Illustrated History of Laredo & Webb County

Historic Lee County: The Story of Fort Myers & Lee County

Historic Louisiana: An Illustrated History

Historic Midland: An Illustrated History

Historic Montgomery County:
An Illustrated History of Montgomery County, Texas

Historic Ocala: The Story of Ocala & Marion County

Historic Oklahoma: An Illustrated History

Historic Oklahoma County: An Illustrated History

Historic Omaha:
An Illustrated History of Omaha and Douglas County

Historic Ouachita Parish: An Illustrated History

Historic Paris and Lamar County: An Illustrated History

Historic Pasadena: An Illustrated History

Historic Passaic County: An Illustrated History

Historic Pennsylvania An Illustrated History

Historic Philadelphia: An Illustrated History

Historic Prescott:
An Illustrated History of Prescott & Yavapai County

Historic Richardson: An Illustrated History

Historic Rio Grande Valley: An Illustrated History

Historic Scottsdale: A Life from the Land

Historic Shelby County: An Illustrated History

Historic Shreveport-Bossier:
An Illustrated History of Shreveport & Bossier City

Historic South Carolina: An Illustrated History

Historic Smith County: An Illustrated History

Historic Temple: An Illustrated History

Historic Texas: An Illustrated History

Historic Victoria: An Illustrated History

Historic Tulsa: An Illustrated History

Historic Williamson County: An Illustrated History

Historic Wilmington & The Lower Cape Fear:
An Illustrated History

Historic York County: An Illustrated History

Iron, Wood & Water: An Illustrated History of Lake Oswego

Jefferson Parish: Rich Heritage, Promising Future

Miami's Historic Neighborhoods: A History of Community

Old Orange County Courthouse: A Centennial History

Plano: An Illustrated Chronicle

The New Frontier:
A Contemporary History of Fort Worth & Tarrant County

The San Gabriel Valley: A 21st Century Portrait

The Spirit of Collin County

Valley Places, Valley Faces

Water, Rails & Oil: Historic Mid & South Jefferson County